The Art of Short Stories
for KS3 and Beyond

Published by Peripeteia Press

First published September 2016

ISBN: 978-0-9954671-18

Peripeteia.webs.com

Contents

Introduction

Like many a story, this book started with us looking for something and not being able to find it. In particular, as English teachers we love sharing great stories with our classes and we were looking for a rich collection of some of the very best stories, ones particularly suitable for key stage 3 pupils. We were looking for a collection of the stories which together form such an integral part of our literary heritage, ideally all lodged in one place. And when our search was in vain, like all protagonists we had to accept defeat or change tack. So instead of just looking for what wasn't there, we had to be a bit more enterprising and actually set about creating it.

We wanted as rich a range as possible. That meant stories from different times and different cultures; Greek stories, Arabian ones, English, Irish and American stories. And we wanted a range of genres; fairy tales and legends, parables and ghost stories, funny ones and wise stories. We also tried to include something familiar and something perhaps new. Hence the less well-known comic story *The Three Wishes* is included alongside *Hansel and Gretel* and the well-known story of Theseus is complemented by the less familiar one of King Pentheus's most unfortunate run-in with the god Bacchus. The stories we've collected also vary in length and in terms of reading difficulty; the shortest is a page and the longest 28 pages. Broadly you'll notice that the stories become progressively more complex in terms of language and content. We imagine some of the opening stories to be more suitable for year 7 classes and some of the later ones for year 9, but hope interested readers of all ages will read across the collection.

We would, of course, have liked a few modern short stories in the mix, but a significant obstacle lay in the way, copyright. As a small independent publisher we couldn't start paying out copyright here, there or, in fact, anywhere. So we confined ourselves to stories already in the public domain, or in some cases we wrote our own version of a classic story.

We hope you enjoy our collection and that it will stimulate you to discover more great stories and find the time to read them with your classes, most particularly your younger classes. Narrative is part of what makes us human, of course. Stories help shape the way we see the world. Stories are cultural artefacts telling us about other times, other people and other places, and they are also vessels carrying timeless wisdom and experience. And, we know you know, but it's still worth saying that stories are also lots of fun, featuring scrapes and fights and adventures and magic, courage and witches and monsters and forests. These stories also come government, time and bomb-proof. Whatever the pressures of assessment and lesson plans and government initiatives we may be navigating, stories are worth sharing whole, most especially the best ones, most especially with children.

Depending on the success or otherwise of this book, we have a second volume in mind with some more fantastic stories. With luck the second volume should be out in the new year. And we'll be setting off on another story.

Neil Bowen & Janice Gearon
September 2016

The Man and the Lion

A man and a lion were travelling together through a forest. They soon began to boast of their superiority to each other in strength and prowess[1]. As they were disputing, they passed a statue carved in stone that represented a Lion strangled by a Man. The traveller pointed to it and said, "See there! Look how strong men are and how we have power even over the Lion, the King of Beasts."

---

[1] Skill or bravery

The Lion replied, "This statue was made by one of you men. If we lions carved statues, you would see the man placed under the paw of the lion."

One story is good until another is told.

The Fox and the Goat

A fox, out walking one morning, fell into a deep well and could find no means of escape. A goat, overcome with thirst, came to the well and, seeing the fox, inquired if the water were good. Concealing his sad plight under a merry guise, the fox indulged in a lavish praise of the water, saying it was excellent beyond measure and encouraging him to descend. The goat, mindful only of his thirst, thoughtlessly jumped down, but, just as he drank, the fox informed him of the difficulty they were both in, and suggested a theme for their common escape. "If," said he, "you will place your forefeet upon the wall and bend your head, I will run up your back and escape, and will help you out afterwards." The goat readily assented and the fox leapt upon his back. Steadying himself with the goat's horns, he safely reached the mouth of the well and made off as fast as he could. When the goat upbraided[2] him for breaking his promise, he turned around and cried out, "You foolish old fellow! If you had as many brains in your head as you have hairs in your beard, you would never have gone down before you had inspected the way up, nor have exposed yourself to dangers from which you had no means of escape!"

Look before you leap.

---

² told off

Theseus and the Minotaur

King Minos of Crete was a powerful man, feared by the rulers of the lands around him. When he demanded goods or men for his great armies, they felt they had to agree. When he demanded they send tributes to honour him, they sent them without question. It was the only way they could stop him going to war with them. But his demands on Athens became too much for them to bear.

King Minos had a great palace built. Inside this palace, Minos had built a giant maze, a Labyrinth, and, at the centre of the maze, he kept a terrifying creature - the Minotaur. Now, this was no ordinary animal; it was a monster: half man; half bull.

It was powerful and savage, and it loved to eat the flesh of the humans who had been shut into the labyrinth by King Minos. They would wander through the maze, completely lost, until at last they came face to face with the Minotaur. Not a great way to die really.

As for Athens, Minos demanded that every year the King send him seven young men and seven young women. 'Why do we send these young people to Crete every year?' Theseus asked his father, the King of Athens. 'And why is it that none of them ever return?'

'Because if we did not send them, Minos would wage war on us and it is a war that we would not win,' said King Aegeus. 'And they do not return because they do not go to Crete as slaves. They go as food for the Minotaur.'

'Father, this is terrible,' shouted Theseus, appalled. 'We cannot let this go on. We cannot sacrifice any more of our young citizens to this tyrant. When it is time to send the next tribute, I will go as one of them and I vow that it is the last time the Minotaur will be fed with the flesh of any of our people.'

Try as he might, his father could not persuade him to change his mind. Aegeus reminded him that every year, other young men had sworn to slay this terrible beast and they had never been seen again. Theseus insisted that he understood the dangers but would succeed. 'I will return to you, father,' called Theseus, as the ship left the harbour wall, 'and you will be proud of your son.'

'Then I wish you good luck, my son,' cried his father, 'I shall keep watch for you every day. If you are successful, take down these black sails and replace them with white ones. That way I will know you are coming home safe to me..'

As the ship docked in Crete, King Minos himself came down to inspect the prisoners from Athens. He enjoyed the chance to taunt the Athenians and to humiliate them even further. 'Is this all your king has to offer this year?' he jeered. 'Such puny creatures. Hardly even a snack for the mighty creature within the labyrinth. Anyway, let's get on with it. I am not a hard-hearted man, so I will let you choose which one goes first into the Minotaur's den. Who is it to be?'

Theseus stepped forward. 'I will go first. I am Theseus, Prince of Athens and I do not fear what is within the walls of your maze.'

'Those are brave words for one so young and so feeble. But the Minotaur will soon have you between its horns. Guards, open the labyrinth and send him in.'

Standing behind the king, listening, was his daughter, Ariadne. From the moment she set eyes on Theseus, Ariadne fell in love with him. As she listened to her father goading and taunting the young prince, she decided that she would help him. As he entered the labyrinth and the guards walked away, she called softly to him. 'Theseus, take this,' she whispered. 'Even if you kill the Minotaur, you will never find your way out again.'

She threw him a great ball of string and he tied one end of it to the entrance. He smiled at her, turned and began to make his way into the maze, the string playing out behind him as he went.

Theseus walked carefully through the dark, foul-smelling passages of the labyrinth, expecting at any moment to come face-to-face with the creature. He did not have long to wait. Turning a corner, with his hands held out in front of him feeling his way, he suddenly touched what felt like a huge bony horn.

In an instant his world turned upside-down, quite literally. He was picked up between the Minotaur's horns and tossed high into the air. When he landed on the hard cold stone, he felt the animal's huge hooves come down on his chest. Every last breath seemed to be knocked out of him and he struggled to stay alive in the darkness.

But Theseus was no ordinary man. He was the son of the King, he

was brave and he was stubborn. As the Minotaur bellowed in his ear and grabbed at him with its hairy arms, Theseus found a strength he did not know he possessed. He grabbed the animal's huge horns, and kept on twisting the great head from side to side. As the animal grew weak, Theseus gave one almighty tug on the head, turning it almost right around. The creature's neck snapped, it gurgled its last breath and fell to the floor with an enormous thud.

It was over; he had done it. The Minotaur was dead. All he had to do was make his way out of...and then he realized the awful truth. In the struggle, he had let go of the string, his lifeline. Theseus felt all over the floor in the pitch darkness. Each time he thought he had found it, he realized that all he had was a long wiry hair from the Minotaur.

Despair set in and Theseus wondered if this was where his life would end, down in the dark, all alone, next to the stinking body. Then, his hand brushed a something and, with a whoop of delight, he knew he had found the thread which would lead him back out. As he neared the entrance of the labyrinth, the darkness began to fade and he made out the figure of Ariadne, waiting for his return.

'You must take me back to Athens with you,' she sobbed. 'My father will kill me when he finds out that I have helped you.'

'But of course you must come with us,' said Theseus. 'It would be cruel to leave you here.' Quickly and quietly, they unfurled the great black sails of their ship and headed for home.

'I cannot believe how my life has changed,' said Ariadne, as they sailed across the calm seas towards Athens. 'To think that I am free of my cruel father and that I will soon be married to a great prince.'

'Married?' echoed Theseus surprised. 'Of course, I owe you a great debt.' But in truth, Theseus did not want to marry Ariadne. So, when their ship docked at an island on their way home, to collect fresh water, Theseus sent Ariadne off to find bread and fruit. The moment she was gone, he set sail and left her on the island. Now, you might think that this was a bad way to reward someone who had helped him and had saved him from certain death. The Gods clearly thought the same thing, for they had a further horror in store for him, as a punishment for his ungrateful treatment of the young girl.

In his haste to get away, Theseus forgot to change his sails to white. King Aegeus, waiting on the headland, saw the ship approaching with its black sails flying in the wind.

'My son has failed and he is dead,' he cried. And in great despair, he flung himself from the cliff into the raging waters below. From that day, the sea was named in memory of Theseus' father, and to this day, is known as the Aegean Sea.

Pentheus and Bacchus

What does the mighty Pentheus, King of Thebes, care if this so-called god, Bacchus has camped at the edge of his kingdom with his band of idiot followers? What does he care of the warnings of that blind old phony, Tiresias? Hadn't Pentheus had the old fool kicked unceremoniously out of his city? And had the great Gods wreaked a terrible vengeance on Pentheus? Of course they had not. The King of Thebes has nothing to fear.

But all too soon the cretinous population of Thebes are streaming out of the city to join Bacchus and his revellers in their drunken riots. Mothers, children, old men, the rich and the poor alike rush to join the new god in his delirious dances. King Pentheus rages and stomps his royal feet and issues terrible threats. But though his words sizzle the air they fall on deaf ears, ears that can only tune into a frantic, irresistible music.

'Guards,' Pentheus screams, 'arrest this upstart Bacchus. Bring him and throw him before my feet.'

When the bruised guards return they are jostling a prisoner roughly between them. But it is not the so-called god, it is just an ordinary Etruscan sailor. And an ugly brute at that. The great King listens to the sailor's story with ill-disguised impatience. A preposterous story about a strange, girlish boy and his terrible revenge on a pack of dim-witted sailors. For such foolishness the mighty King has the sailor dragged off to be tortured on the rack.

But, so it is told, while the torturers prepared their sharp knives and devilish skewers, their heated pincers and extracting tongs, the iron shackles simply fell off the sailor, the bolts of his prison cell simply opened of their own accord and he walked free and unseen from Pentheus's palace.

When the King heard of this, his rage rose to volcanic levels. He would put up with this outrage no longer. It was time he sorted out things himself, once and for all. Enraged, unstoppable, alone, unguarded, King Pentheus climbed mount Clithaeron to tackle the upstart Bacchus with his own hands.

He hears them before he sees them,
the Bacchantes - Bacchus's hordes of
wild revellers. Their drums, their bells,
their cymbals, the stamping of their
feet, their crazy, maddening music,
their shrill exuberant cries and animal
howls reverberate inside Pentheus's skull as his anger twists into
frenzy.

The first to spot the King, where he hides in the undergrowth, is
his own mother. But in her delicious delirium she doesn't see her
son. No, she spots a wild boar. A boar to be attacked and hacked
apart, killed and devoured. Her sharp javelin is the first to pierce
Pentheus's side and soon the whole pack of women pour onto
him, over him, stabbing and ripping and tearing and biting.

It is too late for Pentheus to repent. The god has him writhing in
his jaws, like a rat caught in the teeth of a dog. And Bacchus will
not let go before the lesson is learnt.

'Mother,' Pentheus sobs, 'mother!' But in her bloodlust she cannot
hear him nor see him nor feel the remotest speck of pity for him.

Her eyes, like the eyes of all the frenzied women, are full of blood. Not until, in wild triumph, she finally tears the boar's head from its shoulders does the blood clear from her eyes and she sees the head of her dead son in her gory hands.

Bacchus, the girlish boy god, the sleepy-eyed, soft-cheeked god of wine and dancing and intoxicating[3] pleasure watches on. And smiles.

---

[3] Making drunk

Tir na nÓg

There was once in Ireland a band of brave heroes called the Fianna, and it is known that the leader of the Fianna, Finn MacCumail, had a son named Oisin who was also a member of the Fianna. The Fianna were fierce in battle and sweet tongued, warrior poets in every sense of the word. Oisin was no different.

One day the men of the Fianna were out hunting by the ocean when Finn spotted something rapidly moving across the waves. The men of the Fianna thought it was an invader and began to ready themselves for battle. As the object drew closer the Fianna could only stand by in awe for what they saw was a beautiful woman riding a white horse galloping over the waves. The horse leapt ashore with the woman, and the men knew her to be one of the band of Sidhe. She introduced herself as Niamh, daughter of Manannan Mac Lir, god of the sea, and said she had travelled from Tir na nÓg, the land of eternal youth. The men were entranced by her beauty; by her long golden hair; her fine garments made of silk; and her jewels of gold and precious stones.

Niamh had heard about Oisin and his talent for reciting beautiful poetry, and, gazing on him the first time, immediately fell in love. After a few days in Conemmara, it was time for Niamh to return to

Tir na nÓg, but the thought of leaving Oisin pulled at her heart and so she asked Oisin to come with her, back to Tir na nÓg. Oisin could not refuse. He jumped on the back of Niamh's beautiful white horse, said farewell to his father and fellow warriors, and galloped across the western seas to the land of eternal youth.

It was not long before Oisin and Niamh were married with the

consent of her parents who also loved Oisin very much. They had a family and relished every moment together in this land that knew no pain or sorrow. However after many years Oisin yearned to visit his family and friends in Ireland. Niamh reluctantly agreed to Oisin returning to Conemmara but made him promise never to dismount the horse while there. Oisin promised and kissed her goodbye as she cried for fear that she would never see her beloved husband again.

Oisin drifted across the waves on the back of the great white horse and soon viewed the cliffs of Conemmara in the distance. On reaching the shore Oisin rushed to his family but found their home no longer there. He traveled to Dun Aileann where the Fainna camped, and found the camp covered with weeds. Oisin asked some hunters in the field about Finn and the Fianna, and was told that they'd been dead for hundreds of years. After some confusion Oisin realized what had happened, one day in Tir na nÓg was the same as a year in Ireland, Oisin had been gone for hundreds of years. The only thing for Oisin to do now was travel back to Tir na nÓg and so headed for the coast of Conemarra. On the way he met some hunters struggling to move a large rock and could not bear to watch them struggle so reached down hanging from the saddle to help the hunters. With one last heave Oisin slipped from the saddle and fell to the ground. What the hunters saw drained the blood from their faces and they turned as white as the horse Oisin fell from. Oisin had rapidly aged and crumbled to the ground as dust. With fright the white horse took off and galloped to the west across the ocean back to Tir na nÓg greeting Niamh who trembled with tears knowing she'd never see her beloved Oisin again.

How Morgan Le Fay Tried To Kill King Arthur

KING ARTHUR had a sister called Morgan le Fay, who was skilled in magic of all sorts, and hated her brother because he had slain in battle a Knight whom she loved. But to gain her own ends, and to revenge herself upon the King, she kept a smiling face, and let none guess the passion in her heart.

One day Morgan le Fay went to Queen Guenevere, and asked her leave to go into the country. The Queen wished her to wait till Arthur returned, but Morgan le Fay said she had had bad news and could not wait. Then the Queen let her depart without delay.

Early next morning at break of day Morgan le Fay mounted her horse and rode all day and all night, and at noon next day reached the Abbey of nuns where King Arthur had gone to rest, for he had fought a hard battle, and for three nights had slept but little. 'Do not wake him,' said Morgan le Fay, who had come there knowing she would find him, 'I will rouse him myself when I think he has had enough sleep,' for she thought to steal his sword Excalibur from him. The nuns dared not disobey her, so Morgan le Fay went straight into the room where King Arthur was lying fast asleep in his bed, and in his right hand was grasped his sword Excalibur. When she beheld that sight, her heart fell, for she dared not touch the sword, knowing well that if Arthur waked and saw her she was a dead woman. So she took the scabbard, and went away on horseback.

When the King awoke and missed his scabbard, he was angry, and asked who had been there; and the nuns told him that it was his sister, Morgan le Fay, who had gone away with a scabbard under her mantle. 'Alas!' said Arthur, 'you have watched me badly!'

'Sir,' said they, 'we dared not disobey your sister.'

'Saddle the best horse that can be found,' commanded the King, 'and bid Sir Ontzlake take another and come with me.' And they buckled on their armour and rode after Morgan le Fay.

They had not gone far before they met a cowherd, and they stopped to ask if he had seen any lady riding that way. 'Yes,' said the cowherd, 'a lady passed by here, with forty horses behind her, and went into the forest yonder.' Then they galloped hard till Arthur caught sight of Morgan le Fay, who looked back, and, seeing that it was Arthur who gave chase, pushed on faster than before. And when she saw she could not escape him, she rode into a lake that lay in the plain on the edge of the forest, and, crying out, 'Whatever may befall me, my brother shall not have the scabbard,' she threw the scabbard far into the water, and it sank, for it was heavy with gold and jewels. After that she fled into a valley full of great stones, and turned herself and her men and her horses into blocks of marble. Scarcely had she done this when the King rode up, but seeing her nowhere thought some evil must have befallen her in vengeance for her misdeeds. He then sought high and low for the scabbard, but could not find it, so he returned unto the Abbey.

When Arthur was gone, Morgan le Fay turned herself and her horses and her men back into their former shapes, and said, 'Now, Sirs, we may go where we will.' And she departed into the country of Gore, and made her towns and castles stronger than before, for she feared King Arthur greatly. Meanwhile King Arthur had rested himself at the Abbey, and afterwards he rode to Camelot, and was welcomed by his Queen and all his Knights. And when he told his adventures and how Morgan le Fay sought his death they longed to burn her for her treason.

The next morning there arrived a damsel at the Court with a message from Morgan le Fay, saying that she had sent the King  her brother a rich mantle[4] for a gift, covered with precious stones, and begged him to receive it and to forgive her in whatever she might have offended him. The King answered little, but the mantle pleased him, and he was about to throw it over his shoulders when the lady of the lake stepped forward, and begged that she might speak to him in private. 'What is it?' asked the King. 'Say on here, and fear nothing.' 'Sir,' said the lady, 'do not put on this mantle, or suffer your Knights to put it on, till the bringer of it has worn it in your presence.' 'Your words are wise,' answered the King, 'I will do as you counsel me. Damsel[5], I desire you to put on this mantle that you have brought me, so that I may see it.' 'Sir,' said she, 'it does not become me to wear a King's garment.' 'By my head,' cried Arthur, 'you shall wear it before I put it on my back, or on the back of any of my Knights,' and he signed to them to put it on her, and she fell down dead, burnt to ashes by the enchanted mantle. Then the King was filled with anger, more than he was before, that his sister should have dealt so wickedly by him.

---

[4] cloak
[5] a young unmarried woman

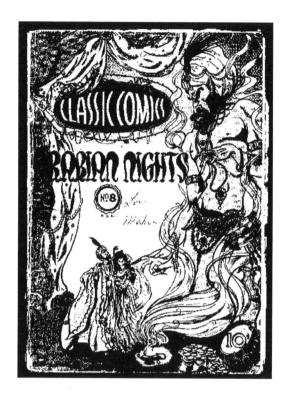

The Story of the Fisherman and the Genie
[part 1]

There was once a very old fisherman, so poor that he could scarcely earn enough to maintain himself, his wife, and three children. Early each morning, he walked to the sea hoping to catch enough fish for himself and his family to eat. He was not a greedy man; he cast his nets no more than four times a day. One morning, he went out so early that his journey was bathed in moonlight. Arriving at the shore, he undressed himself, and cast in his nets. As he drew them towards the beach, he found them very heavy, and rejoiced that he had a good catch of fish. However, when he inspected the catch, he saw that there was nothing in his nets but the carcass of an ass. He heaved a great sad sigh.

After carefully and patiently mending his nets, which the carcass of the ass had broken in several places, he threw them in a second time. Again, when he pulled them out of the water, the nets were so heavy that he believed they were full of fish; this time, however, he found nothing but a basket full of gravel and slime, which caused him to cry out with grief. 'O Fortune!' he wailed in such a lamentable voice. 'Please don't be angry with me. Please don't persecute a poor old man. I came here from my house to seek food for my family. I have no trade but this to live by; and, notwithstanding all the care I take, I can scarcely provide enough to keep them alive.'

Having finished this complaint, and feeling very upset, he threw away the basket. He patiently washed the slime from his nets and cast them a third time. He brought up nothing but stones, shells, and mud. By now, he was almost beside himself with despair. However, when the dawn began to appear, he did not forget to say his prayers, and afterwards

added this petition: 'Lord, you know that I cast my nets only four times a day. I have already drawn them three times, without the least reward for my labour. I will only cast them once more. I pray for the sea to be generous to me.'

Having finished his prayer, the fisherman cast his nets for the fourth time. When he thought the time was right, he drew them as before, with great difficulty. Instead of fish, he found nothing in them but a vessel of yellow copper, which, by its weight, seemed to be full of something. He noticed that it had been carefully sealed with lead and stamped with an elaborate design. All his sadness disappeared in an instant. 'I will sell it,' he declared, 'at the foundry, and, with the money, buy a measure of corn.' He examined the vessel on all sides, and shook it, to see if what was inside made any noise but heard nothing. This, with the impression of the seal upon the leaden cover, made him think there was something precious in it. Desperate to know what was inside, he took a knife and opened it with very little trouble. He turned the vessel upside down, but surprisingly nothing fell out. He set it before him, and while he carefully examined it, a thick silvery grey smoke emerged which obliged him to step back two or three paces.

The smoke ascended to the clouds, and extending itself along the sea and upon the shore, formed a great mist, which, we may well imagine, astonished the fisherman who watched its movement awestruck. When the smoke was all out of the vessel, it gathered together, and became a solid body - a genie twice as high as the greatest of giants. At the sight of such a monster, the fisherman would have fled, but terror rooted him to the spot.

'Solomon,' boomed the genie, 'Solomon, great prophet, forgive me; I will never more oppose your will. I will obey all your commands.'

When the fisherman heard these words of the genie, he gathered his courage, and spoke. 'Proud spirit, what is it that you say? It is above eighteen hundred years since the prophet Solomon died, and we are now at the end of time. Tell me your history, and how you came to be shut up in this vessel.'

The genie, turning to the fisherman with a fierce look, said, 'You must speak to me with more civility[6]. You are too bold to call me a proud spirit. If you do not speak to me with more respect, I will kill you in an instant.'

---

[6] politeness

'Ah!' replied the fisherman. 'Why would you kill me? Did I not just now set you at liberty, and have you already forgotten it?'

'Of course I remember,' the genie roared,' but that shall not deter me from killing you. But first, I must grant you one favour.'

'And what is that?' asked the fisherman.

'It is,' answered the genie, 'to give you a choice. You must decide in what manner you wish me to take your life.'

'But what have I done to offend you so badly?' begged the fisherman. 'Is that your reward for the good service I have done you?'

'I cannot treat you otherwise,' said the genie. 'Listen to my story and you will understand.

I am one of those rebellious spirits that opposed the will of Heaven. All the other genii obeyed Solomon, the great prophet, loyally. They did whatever he asked of them. Sacar and I were the only genii that refused to do anything unkind and we disobeyed the orders of Solomon. To avenge himself, that great monarch sent Asaph, the son of his chief minister, to capture me. Asaph succeeded and brought me cruelly by force before his master's throne.

'Solomon, the son of David, commanded me to change my beliefs, to acknowledge his power, and to submit myself to his commands: I bravely refused to obey, and told him I would rather suffer his anger than swear loyalty and service to him, as he required. To punish me, he shut me up in this copper vessel; and to make sure that I should not break out of this prison, he himself stamped his seal upon this lead cover. Then he gave the vessel to one of his loyal genii with orders to throw me into the sea, which was done, to my great sorrow.

'During the first hundred years' imprisonment, I swore that if anyone released me before the hundred years had passed, I would make him rich, but that century ran out, and nobody found me. During the second, I made an oath that I would open all the treasures of the earth to anyone who set me free, but with no better success. In the third, I promised to make my saviour a powerful ruler, and to grant him, every day, three wishes, but this century ran out as well and I continued in my prison. At last, driven almost mad at finding myself a prisoner for so long, I swore that if anyone should free me, I would kill him without mercy, and grant him no other favour but to choose what his manner of death. Therefore, since you have delivered me to-day, I give you that choice.'

This tale upset the poor fisherman beyond measure. 'I am very unfortunate,' he lamented, 'to have done such a piece of good service to someone who is so ungrateful. I beg you to reconsider. Pardon me, and heaven will pardon you; if you grant me my life, heaven will protect you from all attempts against yours.'

'No, I have decided,' declared the genie, 'You must choose how you will die.'

The fisherman, seeing the genie to be determined, was terribly downhearted, not so much for himself as for his three children, and the misery they must be reduced to by his death. He tried again to appease the genie, and sobbed, 'Alas! Please take pity on me. Consider the good service I have done you.'

'I have told you already,' replied the genie, 'it is for that very reason I must kill you.'

'That is very strange,' said the fisherman. 'Are you really resolved to reward good with evil? The proverb says, "He who does good to one who deserves it not is always ill rewarded." I must confess I thought it was false; for in reality there can be nothing more contrary to reason, or to the laws of society. Nevertheless, I find now by cruel experience that it is but too true.'

'Do not waste time,' replied the genie. 'All your talking will not divert me from my purpose. Hurry up and tell me which way you choose to die.'

Necessity is surely the mother of invention. The fisherman thought of a wily plan. 'Since I must die then, I submit to the will of heaven; but, before I choose the manner of death, I conjure you, by the great name which was engraved upon the seal of the prophet Solomon, to answer me truly the question I am going to ask you.'

The genie yawned, 'Ask what you want, but do hurry up.'

The genie having promised to speak the truth, the fisherman said to him, 'I wish to know if you were actually in this vessel.'

'Yes,' replied the genie, 'I swear that I was; and it is a certain truth.'

'In good faith,' answered the fisherman calmly, ' I cannot believe you. The vessel is not capable of holding one of your great size. How is it possible that your whole body could fit in it?'

'I swear,' replied the genie, 'that I was there just as now see me here. Is it possible that you don't believe me after this great oath that I have taken?'

'Truly, I do not,' said the fisherman holding out the vessel; 'nor will I believe you unless you show me.'

In an instant, the body of the genie dissolved and changed itself into smoke, extending above the sea and shore. It gathered together and, swirling and coiling smoothly and precisely, it re-entered the vessel, until not a wisp was left. A small voice called out to the fisherman, 'Well, incredulous fellow, I am all in the vessel. Do not you believe me now?'

The fisherman, instead of answering the genie, took the cover and speedily jammed the vessel shut. 'Genie,' cried he, 'now it is your turn to beg my favour, and to choose which way I shall put you to death. Perhaps I should throw you back into the sea. I could build a house upon the bank, where I will live, and warn all fishermen who come to throw in their nets to beware of such a wicked genie as you, with your oath to kill anyone who sets you free.'

The genie, enraged, did all he could to get out of the vessel again; but it was all in vain. So, realising that the fisherman had the advantage of him, he decided to try a different approach. 'Fisherman,' said he, in a much more pleasant tone, 'please reconsider. What I said earlier was just a joke, and you mustn't take it any other way.'

'Oh genie!' replied the fisherman, 'a moment ago you were the greatest of all genii, and now are the least of them. Your craftiness is obvious. Back to the sea with you. If you've been there as long as you say then you might as well stay there till the day of judgment. I begged you, in God's name, not to take away my life, and rejected my prayers. Thus, I must treat you in the same manner.'

The genie did his very best to persuade the fisherman. 'Open the vessel,' he wailed. 'Please give me my liberty and I promise to give you anything you wish.'

'You are an untrustworthy traitor,' snapped the fisherman. 'I should deserve to lose my life if I were such a fool as to believe you.'

'My good, dear, kind, best friend,' replied the genie, 'I implore you once more not to be guilty of such cruelty. Think about it. It is not good to take revenge. If you do, you will be no better than Imama who treated Ateca so badly.'

'What did Imama do to Ateca?' replied the fisherman.

'Ho!' said the genie, 'if you want to hear this great story, open the vessel. Do you think that I can be in a humour to tell stories in so tiny a prison? I will tell you as many as you please when you let me out.'

'No,' said the fisherman, 'I will not let you out. I am just going to throw you to the bottom of the sea.'

'Hear me one word more,' cried the genie. ' I promise to do you no harm. Instead I will show you how to become exceedingly rich.'

The hope of delivering himself from poverty won over the fisherman.

'I might listen to you,' said he, 'were there any credit to be given to your word. Swear to me by the Great Name that you will faithfully perform what you promise, and I will open the vessel. I do not believe you will dare to break such an oath.'

The genie swore to him, and the fisherman immediately took off the covering of the vessel. At that very instant the smoke came out, and the genie, having resumed his form as before, kicked the vessel straight into the sea. This action frightened the fisherman.

'Genie,' said he, 'what is the meaning of that? Will you not keep the oath you just now made?'

The genie laughed at the fisherman's fear, and answered: 'Oh, don't be afraid; I only did it to please myself. To persuade you that I am in earnest, take your nets and follow me.' As he spoke these words, he walked before the fisherman, who took up his nets, and followed him, but with some distrust. They passed by the town, and came to the top of a mountain, then down into a vast plain, and presently to a great pond that lay between four hills.

When they came to the side of the pond, the genie said to the fisherman, 'Cast your nets and catch fish.' The fisherman did not doubt of catching some, because he saw a great number in the pond; but he was extremely surprised when he found that they were of four colours--white, red, blue, and yellow. He threw in his nets, and brought out one of each colour. Having never seen the like, he could not but admire them, and, judging that he might get a considerable sum for them, he was very joyful.

'Carry those fish,' said the genie, 'and present them to the sultan; he will give you more money for them than ever you had in your life. You may come every day to fish in this pond. But listen well, I give you warning not to throw in your nets above once a day, otherwise you will regret it. Take heed, and remember my advice.' Having spoken thus, he struck his foot upon the ground, which opened and him swallowed up.

The fisherman did as he was told and returned to the town very well satisfied with his fish. He went straight to the sultan's luxurious palace.

The sultan was very surprised when he saw the four fishes. He took them up one after another, and looked at them carefully. After having admired them a long time, he said to his first vizier, 'Take these fishes to the chef. I am sure they will taste unlike any other fish I have eaten.' The sultan then ordered his second vizier[7] to give the fisherman four hundred pieces of gold coin.

The fisherman, who had never seen so much cash in his lifetime, could scarcely believe his own good fortune. He didn't waste a single coin but spent it very wisely upon his now happy, well-fed family.

---

[7] a high ranking official of the court

Hansel and Gretel

The Brothers Grimm, 1812

Near a great forest there lived a poor woodcutter with his wife and his two children; the boy's name was Hansel and the girl's Gretel. They had very little to bite or to sup, and once, when there was great dearth in the land, the man could not even provide the daily bread. As he lay in bed one night thinking of this, and turning and tossing, he sighed heavily, and said to his wife, "What will become of us? We cannot even feed our children; there is nothing left for ourselves."

"I will tell you what, husband," answered the wife; "we will take the children early in the morning into the forest, where it is thickest; we will make them a fire, and we will give each of them a piece of bread. Then we will go to our work and leave them alone; they will never find the way home again, and we shall be quit of them."

"No, wife," said the man, "I cannot do that; I cannot find in my heart to take my children into the forest and to leave them there alone; the wild animals would soon come and devour them."

"O you fool," said she, "then we will all four starve; you had better get the coffins ready"- and she left him no peace until he consented.

"But I really pity the poor children," said the man. The two children had not been able to sleep for hunger, and had heard what their step-mother had said to their father.

Gretel wept bitterly, and said to Hansel, "It is all over with us."

"Do be quiet, Gretel," said Hansel, "and do not fret. I will manage something." And when the parents had gone to sleep he got up, put on his little coat, opened the back door, and slipped out. The moon was shining brightly, and the white flints that lay in front of the house glistened like pieces of silver. Hansel stooped and filled the little pocket of his coat as full as it would hold. Then he went back again, and said to Gretel, "Be easy, dear little sister, and go to sleep quietly; God will not forsake us," and laid himself down again in his bed.

When the day was breaking, and before the sun had risen, the wife came and awakened the two children, saying, "Get up, you lazy bones; we are going into the forest to cut wood." Then she gave each of them a piece of bread, and said, "That is for dinner, and you must not eat it before then, for you will get no more."

Gretel carried the bread under her apron, for Hansel had his pockets full of the flints. Then they set off all together on their way to the forest. When they had gone a little way Hansel stood still and looked back towards the house, and this he did again and again, till his father said to him, "Hansel, what are you looking at? Take care not to forget your legs."

"O father," said Hansel, "I am looking at my little white kitten, who is sitting up on the roof to bid me good-bye."

"You young fool," said the woman, "that is not your kitten, but the sunshine on the chimney pot." Of course Hansel had not been looking at his kitten, but had been taking every now and then a flint from his pocket and dropping it on the road.

When they reached the middle of the forest the father told the children to collect wood to make a fire to keep them warm; and Hansel and Gretel gathered brushwood enough for a little mountain; and it was set on fire, and when the flame was burning quite high the wife said, "Now lie down by the fire and rest yourselves, you children, and we will go and cut wood; and when we are ready we will come and fetch you." So Hansel and Gretel sat by the fire, and at noon they each ate their pieces of bread. They  thought their father was in the wood all the time, as they seemed to hear the strokes of the axe, but really it was only a dry branch hanging to a withered tree that the wind moved to and fro. So when they had stayed there a long time their eyelids closed with weariness, and they fell fast asleep.

When at last they woke it was night, and Gretel began to cry, and said, "How shall we ever get out of this wood?"

But Hansel comforted her, saying, "Wait a little while longer, until the moon rises, and then we can easily find the way home." And when the full moon got up Hansel took his little sister by the hand, and followed the way where the flint stones shone like silver, and showed them the road. They walked on the whole night through, and at the break of day they came to their father's house. They knocked at the door, and when the wife opened it and saw it was Hansel and Gretel she said, "You naughty children, why did you sleep so long in the wood? We thought you were never coming home again!" But the father was glad, for it had gone to his heart to leave them both in the woods alone.

Not very long after that there was again great scarcity in those parts, and the children heard their mother say at night in bed to their father, "Everything is finished up; we have only half a loaf, and after that the tale comes to an end. The children must be off; we will take them farther into the wood this time, so that they shall not be able to find the way back again; there is no other way to manage." The man felt sad at heart, and he thought, "It would be better to share one's last morsel with one's children." But the wife would listen to nothing that he said, but scolded and reproached him. But the children were not asleep, and had heard all the talk.

When the parents had gone to sleep Hansel got up to go out and get more flint stones, as he did before, but the wife had locked the door, and Hansel could not get out; but he comforted his little sister, and said, "Don't cry, Gretel, and go to sleep quietly, and God will help us."

Early the next morning the wife came and pulled the children out of bed. She gave them each a little piece of bread- less than before; and on the way to the wood Hansel crumbled the bread in his pocket, and often stopped to throw a crumb on the ground. "Hansel, what are you stopping behind and staring for?" said the father.

"I am looking at my little pigeon sitting on the roof, to say good-bye to me," answered Hansel.

"You fool," said the wife, "that is no pigeon, but the morning sun shining on the chimney pots." Hansel went on as before, and strewed breadcrumbs all along the road.

The woman led the children far into the wood, where they had never been before in all their lives. And again there was a large fire made, and the mother said, "Sit still there, you children, and when you are tired you can go to sleep; we are going into the forest to cut wood, and in the evening, when we are ready to go home we will come and fetch you." So when noon came Gretel shared her bread with

Hansel, who had strewed his along the road. Then they went to sleep, and the evening passed, and no one came for the poor children. When they awoke it was dark night, and Hansel comforted his little sister, and said, "Wait a little, Gretel, until the moon gets up, then we shall be able to see the way home by the crumbs of bread that I have scattered along it."

So when the moon rose they got up, but they could find no crumbs of bread, for the birds of the woods and of the fields had come and picked them up. Hansel thought they might find the way all the same, but they could not. They went on all that night, and the next day from the morning until the evening, but they could not find the way out of the wood, and they were very hungry, for they had nothing to eat but the few berries they could pick up. And when they were so tired that they could no longer drag themselves along, they lay down under a tree and fell asleep.

It was now the third morning since they had left their father's house. They were always trying to get back to it, but instead of that they only found themselves farther in the wood, and if help had not soon come they would have starved. About noon they saw a pretty snow-white bird sitting on a bough, and singing so sweetly that they stopped to listen. And when he had finished the bird spread his wings and flew before them, and they followed after him until they came to a little house, and the bird perched on the roof, and when they came nearer they saw that the house was built of bread, and roofed with cakes, and the window was of transparent sugar.

"We will have some of this," said Hansel, "and make a fine meal. I will eat a piece of the roof, Gretel, and you can have some of the window - that will taste sweet." So Hansel reached up and broke off a bit of the roof, just to see how it tasted, and Gretel stood by the window and gnawed at it.

Then they heard a thin voice call out from inside, "Nibble, nibble, like a mouse, Who is nibbling at my house?"

And the children answered, "Never mind, It is the wind." And they went on eating, never disturbing themselves. Hansel, who found that the roof tasted very nice, took down a great piece of it, and

Gretel pulled out a large round window pane, and sat her down and began upon it. Then the door opened, and an aged woman came out, leaning upon a crutch. Hansel and Gretel felt very frightened, and let fall what they had in their hands.

The old woman, however, nodded her head, and said, "Ah, my dear children, how come you here? You must come indoors and stay with me, you will be no trouble." So she took them each by the hand, and led them into her little house. And there they found a good meal laid out, of milk and pancakes, with sugar, apples, and nuts. After that she showed them two little white beds, and Hansel and Gretel laid themselves down on them, and thought they were in heaven.

The old woman, although her behaviour was so kind, was a wicked witch, who lay in wait for children, and had built the little house on purpose to entice them. When they were once inside she used to kill them, cook them, and eat them, and then it was a feast-day with her. The witch's eyes were red, and she could not see very far, but she had a keen scent, like the beasts, and knew very well when human creatures were near. When she knew that

Hansel and Gretel were coming, she gave a spiteful laugh, and said triumphantly, "I have them, and they shall not escape me!"

Early in the morning, before the children were awake, she got up to look at them, and as they lay sleeping so peacefully with round rosy cheeks, she said to herself, "What a fine feast I shall have!" Then she grasped Hansel with her withered hand, and led him into a little stable, and shut him up behind a grating; and call and scream as he might, it was no good. Then she went back to Gretel and shook her, crying, "Get up, lazy bones; fetch water, and cook something nice for your brother; he is outside in the stable, and must be fattened up. And when he is fat enough I will eat him."

Gretel began to weep bitterly, but it was no use, she had to do what the wicked witch bade her. And so the best kind of victuals was cooked for poor Hansel, while Gretel got nothing but crab-shells. Each morning the old woman visited the little stable, and cried, "Hansel, stretch out your finger, that I may tell if you will soon be fat enough." Hansel, however, used to hold out a little bone, and the old woman, who had weak eyes, could not see what it was, and supposing it to be Hansel's finger, wondered very much that it was not getting fatter.

When four weeks had passed and Hansel seemed to remain so thin, she lost patience and could wait no longer. "Now then, Gretel," cried she to the little girl; "be quick and draw water; be Hansel fat or be he lean, tomorrow I must kill and cook him." Oh what a grief for the poor little sister to have to fetch water, and how the tears flowed down over her cheeks!

"Dear God, pray help us!" cried she; "if we had been devoured by wild beasts in the wood at least we should have died together."
"Spare me your lamentations[8]," said the old woman; "they are of no avail."

Early next morning Gretel had to get up, make the fire, and fill the kettle. "First we will do the baking," said the old woman; "I have heated the oven already, and kneaded the dough." She pushed poor Gretel towards the oven, out of which the flames were already shining. "Creep in," said the witch, "and see if it is properly hot, so that the bread may be baked." And Gretel once in, she meant to shut the door upon her and let her be baked, and then she would have eaten her.

But Gretel perceived her intention, and said, "I don't know how to do it; how shall I get in?"
"Stupid goose," said the old woman, "the opening is big enough,

---

[8] cries of unhappiness

do you see? I could get in myself!" and she stooped down and put her head in the oven's mouth. Then Gretel gave her a push, so that she went in farther, and she shut the iron door upon her, and put up

the bar. Oh how frightfully she howled! But Gretel ran away, and left the wicked witch to burn miserably. Gretel went straight to Hansel, opened the stable-

door, and cried, "Hansel, we are free! The old witch is dead!" Then out flew Hansel like a bird from its cage as soon as the door is opened.

How rejoiced they both were! How they fell each on the other's neck and danced about, and kissed each other! And as they had nothing more to fear they went over all the old witch's house, and in every corner there stood chests of pearls and precious stones. "This is something better than flint stones," said Hansel, as he filled his pockets; and Gretel, thinking she also would like to carry something home with her, filled her apron full. "Now, away we go," said Hansel, "if we only can get out of the witch's wood."

When they had journeyed a few hours they came to a great piece of water. "We can never get across this," said Hansel, "I see no stepping-stones and no bridge."

"And there is no boat either," said Gretel; "but here comes a white duck; if I ask her she will help us over." So she cried, "Duck, duck, here we stand, Hansel and Gretel, on the land, Stepping-stones and bridge we lack, Carry us over on your nice white back." And the duck came accordingly, and Hansel got upon her and told his sister to come too. "No," answered Gretel, "that would be too hard upon the duck; we can go separately, one after the other."

And that was how it was managed, and after that they went on happily, until they came to the wood, and the way grew more and more familiar, till at last they saw in the distance their father's house. Then they ran till they came up to it, rushed in at the door, and fell on their father's neck. The man had not had a quiet hour since he left his children in the wood; but the wife was dead. And when Gretel opened her apron the pearls and precious stones were scattered all over the room, and Hansel took one handful after another out of his pocket. Then was all care at an end, and they lived in great joy together.

The Three Wishes

Once upon a time . . . a woodcutter lived happily with his wife in a pretty little log cabin in the middle of a thick forest. Each morning he set off singing to work, and when he came home in the evening, a plate of hot steaming soup was always waiting for him.   One day, however, he had a strange surprise. He came upon a big fir tree with strange open holes on the trunk. It looked somehow different from the other trees, and just as he was about to chop it down, the alarmed face of an elf popped out of a hole.

 "What's all this banging?" asked the elf. "You're not thinking of cutting down this tree, are you? It's my home. I live here!" The woodcutter dropped his axe in astonlshment. "Well, I . . ." he stammered. "With all the other trees there are in this forest, you have to pick this one. Lucky I was in, or I would have found myself homeless." Taken aback at these words, the woodcutter quickly recovered, for after all the elf was quite tiny, while he himself was a big hefty chap, and he boldly replied: "I'll cut down any tree I like, so . . ."

"All right! All right!" broke in the elf. "Shall we put it this way: if you don't cut down this tree, I grant you three wishes. Agreed?" The woodcutter scratched his head. "Three wishes, you say? Yes, I agree." And he began to hack at another tree. As he worked and sweated at his task, the woodcutter kept thinking about the magic wishes. "I'll see what my wife thinks..."

The woodcutter's wife was busily cleaning a pot outside the house when her husband arrived. Grabbing her round the waist, he twirled her in delight. "Hooray! Hooray! Our luck is in!" The woman could not understand why her husband was so pleased with himself and she shrugged herself free. Later, however, over a glass of fine wine at the table, the woodcutter told his wife of his meeting with the elf, and she too began to picture the wonderful things that the elf's three wishes might give them. The woodcutter's wife took a first sip of wine from her husband's glass. "Nice," she said, smacking her lips. "I wish I had a string of sausages to go with it, though..." Instantly she bit her tongue, but too late.

Out of the air appeared the sausages while the woodcutter stuttered with rage. ". . . what have you done! Sausages . . . What a stupid waste of a wish! You foolish woman. I wish they would stick up your nose!" No sooner said than done. For the sausages leapt up and stuck fast to the end of the woman's nose. This time, the woodcutter's wife flew into a rage. "You idiot, what have you done?

With all the things we could have wished for . . ." The mortified woodcutter, who had just repeated his wife's own mistake, exclaimed: "I'd chop . . ." Luckily he stopped himself in time, realizing with horror that he'd been on the point of having his tongue chopped off. As his wife complained and blamed him, the poor man burst out laughing. "If only you knew how funny you look with those sausages on the end of your nose!" Now that really upset the woodcutter's wife. She hadn't thought of her looks. She tried to tug away the sausages but they would not budge. She pulled again and again, but in vain. The sausages were firmly attached to her nose. Terrified, she exclaimed: "They'll be there for the rest of my life!" Feeling sorry for his wife and wondering how he could ever put up with a woman with such an awkward nose, the woodcutter said: "I'll try." Grasping the string of sausages, he tugged with all his might. But he simply pulled his wife over on top of him. The pair sat on the floor, gazing sadly at each other.

"What shall we do now?" they said, each thinking the same thought. "There's only one thing we can do . . ." ventured the woodcutter's wife timidly. "Yes, I'm afraid so . . ." her husband sighed, remembering their dreams of riches, and he bravely wished the third and last wish "I wish the sausages would leave my wife's nose." And they did. Instantly, husband and wife hugged each other tearfully, saying "Maybe we'll be poor, but we'll be happy again!"

That evening, the only reminder of the woodcutter's meeting with the elf was the string of sausages. So the couple fried them, gloomily thinking of what that meal had cost them.

The Legend of Sleepy Hollow

Washington Irving, 1820

In the bosom of one of those spacious coves which indent the eastern shore of the Hudson, at that broad expansion of the river denominated[9] by the ancient Dutch navigators the Tappan Zee, and where they always prudently shortened sail and implored the protection of Saint Nicholas, there lies a small market town which is generally known by the name of Tarry Town. This name was given by the good housewives of the adjacent country from the inveterate propensity[10] of their husbands to linger about the village tavern on market days. Not far from this village, perhaps about two miles,

---

[9] named
[10] bad habit or tendency

there is a little valley among high hills which is one of the quietest places in the whole world. A small brook murmurs through it and, with the occasional whistle of a quail or tapping of a woodpecker, is almost the only sound that ever breaks the uniform tranquillity.

From the listless repose of the place, this sequestered[11] glen has long been known by the name of Sleepy Hollow. Some say that the place was bewitched during the early days of the Dutch settlement; others, that an old Indian chief, the wizard of his tribe, held his powwows there before the country was discovered by Master Hendrick Hudson. Certain it is, the place still continues under the sway of some witching power that holds a spell over the minds of the descendants of the original settlers. They are given to all kinds of marvelous beliefs, are subject to trances and visions, and frequently hear music and voices in the air. The whole neighborhood abounds with local tales, haunted spots, and twilight superstitions.

The dominant spirit that haunts this enchanted region is the apparition of a figure on horseback without a head. It is said to be the ghost of a Hessian trooper, whose head had been carried away by a cannonball in some nameless battle during the Revolutionary War, and who is ever seen by the countryfolk, hurrying along in the gloom of the night as if on the wings of the wind. Historians of those parts allege that the body of the trooper having been buried in the

---

[11] hidden

yard of a church at no great distance, the ghost rides forth to the scene of battle in nightly quest of his head; and that the rushing speed with which he sometimes passes along the Hollow is owing to his being in a hurry to get back to the churchyard before daybreak. The specter is known, at all the country firesides, by the name of the Headless Horseman of Sleepy Hollow.

2

It is remarkable that this visionary propensity is not confined to native inhabitants of this little retired Dutch valley, but is unconsciously imbibed[12] by everyone who resides there for a time. However wide-awake they may have been before they entered that sleepy region, they are sure, in a little time, to inhale the witching influence of the air and begin to grow imaginative, to dream dreams, and see apparitions.

In this by-place of nature there abode, some thirty years since, a worthy wight [13] of the name of Ichabod Crane, a native of Connecticut, who "tarried" in Sleepy Hollow for the purpose of instructing the children of the vicinity. He was tall and exceedingly lank, with narrow shoulders, long arms and legs, hands that dangled a mile out of his sleeves, and feet that might have served for

---

[12] drunk
[13] man

shovels. His head was small, and flat at top, with huge ears, large green glassy eyes, and a long snipe nose, so that it looked like a weathercock perched upon his spindle neck, to tell which way the wind blew. To see him striding along on a windy day, with his clothes bagging and fluttering about him, one might have mistaken him for some scarecrow eloped from a cornfield.

His schoolhouse was a low building of one large room, rudely constructed of logs. It stood in a rather lonely but pleasant situation, just at the foot of a woody hill, with a brook running close by, and a formidable birch tree growing at one end of it. From hence the low murmur of his pupils' voices, conning over their lessons, might be heard on a drowsy summer's day, interrupted now and then by the voice of the master in a tone of menace or command; or by the appalling sound of the birch as he urged some wrongheaded Dutch urchin along the flowery path of knowledge. All this he called "doing his duty," and he never inflicted a chastisement[14] without following it by the assurance, so consolatory to the smarting urchin, that "he would remember it, and thank him for it the longest day he had to live."

When school hours were over, Ichabod was even the companion and playmate of the larger boys; and on holiday afternoons would convoy some of the smaller ones home, who happened to have

---

[14] punishment

pretty sisters, or good housewives for mothers, noted for the comforts of the cupboard. Indeed it behooved him to keep on good terms with his pupils. The revenue arising from his school would have been scarcely sufficient to furnish him with daily bread, for he was a huge feeder and, though lank, had the dilating powers of an anaconda. To help out his maintenance he was, according to custom in those parts, boarded and lodged at the homes of his pupils a week at a time; thus going the rounds of the neighborhood, with all his worldly effects tied up in a cotton handkerchief.

3

That this might not be too onerous[15] for his rustic patrons, he assisted the farmers occasionally by helping to make hay, mending the fences, and driving the cows from pasture. He laid aside, too, all the dominant dignity with which he lorded it in the school, and became wonderfully gentle and ingratiating. He found favor in the eyes of the mothers by petting the children, particularly the youngest, and he would sit with a child on one knee, and rock a cradle with his foot for whole hours together.

In addition to his other vocations, he was the singing master of the neighborhood, and picked up many bright shillings by instructing the young folks in psalmody[16]. Thus, by divers little makeshifts, the worthy pedagogue got on tolerably enough and was thought, by all who understood nothing of the labor of headwork, to have a wonderfully easy life of it.

The schoolmaster is generally a man of some importance in the female circle of a rural neighborhood, being considered a kind of idle, gentlemanlike personage, of vastly superior taste and accomplishments to the rough country swains. How he would figure among the country damsels in the churchyard, between services on Sundays! - gathering grapes for them from the wild vines that

---

[15] requiring great effort
[16] singing psalms

overran the surrounding trees; reciting for their amusement all the epitaphs on the tombstones; while the more bashful bumpkins hung sheepishly back, envying his superior elegance and address.

He was, moreover, esteemed by the women as a man of great erudition[17], for he had read several books quite through, and was a perfect master of Cotton Mather's 'History of New England Witchcraft'. His appetite for the marvelous was extraordinary. It was often his delight, after his school was dismissed, to stretch himself on the clover bordering the little brook and there con over old Mather's direful tales in the gathering dusk. Then, as he wended his way to the farmhouse where he happened to be quartered, every sound of nature, the boding cry of the tree toad, the dreary hooting of the screech owl, fluttered his excited imagination. His only resource on such occasions was to sing psalm tunes; and the good people of Sleepy Hollow were often filled with awe at hearing his nasal melody floating along the dusky road.

4

Another of his sources of fearful pleasure was to pass long winter evenings with the old Dutch wives, as they sat spinning by the fire, with a row of apples roasting and spluttering along the hearth, and listen to their marvelous tales of ghosts and goblins, haunted

---

[17] great knowledge

bridges and haunted houses, and particularly of the headless horseman. But if there was a pleasure in all this while snugly cuddling in the chimney corner, it was dearly purchased by the terrors of his subsequent walk homeward. How often did he shrink with curdling awe at some rushing blast, howling among the trees of a snowy night, in the idea that it was the Galloping Hessian of the Hollow!

All these, however, were mere phantoms of the dark. Daylight put mend to all these evils. He would have passed a pleasant life of it if his path had not been crossed by a being that causes more perplexity to mortal man than ghosts, goblins, and the whole race of witches put together, and that was -- a woman.

Among the musical disciples who assembled, one evening in each week, to receive his instructions in psalmody was Katrina Van Tassel, the only child of a substantial Dutch farmer. She was a blooming lass of fresh eighteen, plump as a partridge, ripe and melting and rosy-cheeked as one of her father's peaches, and universally famed, not merely for her beauty, but her vast expectations. She was withal a little of a coquette[18], as might be perceived in her dress. She wore ornaments of pure yellow gold to set off her charms, and a provokingly short petticoat to display the prettiest foot and ankle in the country round.

---

[18] flirt

Ichabod Crane had a soft and foolish heart toward the sex; and it is not to be wondered at that so tempting a morsel soon found favor in his eyes, more especially after he had visited her in her paternal mansion. Old Baltus Van Tassel was a perfect picture of a thriving, contented, liberal-hearted farmer. He seldom, it is true, sent either his eyes or his thoughts beyond the boundaries of his own farm; but within those everything was snug, happy, and abundant.

Baltus Van Tassel

5

The Van Tassel stronghold was situated on the banks of the Hudson, in one of those green, sheltered, fertile nooks in which the Dutch farmers are so fond of nestling. A great elm tree spread its broad branches over it, at the foot of which bubbled up a spring of the softest and sweetest water. Hard by the farmhouse was a vast barn, every window and crevice of which seemed bursting forth with the treasures of the farm. Rows of pigeons were enjoying the sunshine on the roof. Sleek unwieldy porkers were grunting in the repose and abundance of their pens. A stately squadron of snowy geese were riding in an adjoining pond, convoying whole fleets of ducks; regiments of turkeys were gobbling through the farmyard.

The pedagogue's [19] mouth watered as he looked upon this sumptuous promise of luxurious winter fare. In his devouring mind's eye he pictured to himself every roasting pig running about with an apple in his mouth; the pigeons were snugly put to bed in a comfortable pie, and tucked in with a coverlet of crust.

As the enraptured Ichabod fancied all this, and as he rolled his great green eyes over the fat meadowlands, the rich fields of wheat, rye, buckwheat, and Indian corn, and the orchard, burdened with ruddy fruit, which surrounded the warm tenement of Van Tassel, his heart yearned after the damsel who was to inherit these domains, and his imagination expanded with the idea how they might be readily turned into cash, and the money invested in immense tracts

---

[19] teacher

of wild land, and shingle palaces in the wilderness. His busy fancy already presented to him the blooming Katrina, with a whole family of children, mounted on the top of a wagon loaded with household trumpery[20]; and he beheld himself bestriding a pacing mare, with a colt at her heels, setting out for Kentucky, Tennessee, or the Lord knows where.

When he entered the house, the conquest of his heart was complete. It was one of those spacious farmhouses, with high-ridged but low-sloping roofs, built in the style handed down from the first Dutch settlers, the projecting eaves forming a piazza along the front. From the piazza the wondering Ichabod entered the hall, which formed the center of the mansion. Here, rows of resplendent pewter, ranged on a long dresser, dazzled his eyes. In one corner stood a huge bag of wool ready to be spun; ears of Indian corn and strings of dried apples and peaches hung in gay festoons along the walls; and a door left ajar gave him a peep into the best parlor, where the claw-footed chairs and dark mahogany tables shone like mirrors. Mock oranges and conch shells decorated the mantelpiece; strings of various colored birds' eggs were suspended above it, and a corner cupboard, knowingly left open, displayed immense treasures of old silver and well-mended china.

---

[20] bits and bobs

6

From the moment Ichabod laid his eyes upon these regions of delight, the peace of his mind was at an end, and his only study was how to win the heart of the peerless daughter of Van Tassel. In this enterprise, however, he had to encounter a host of rustic admirers, who kept a watchful and angry eye upon each other, but were ready to fly out in the common cause against any new competitor. Among these the most formidable was a burly, roaring, roistering blade of the name of Brom Van Brunt, the hero of the country round, which rang with his feats of strength and hardihood. He was broad-shouldered, with short curly black hair, and a bluff but not unpleasant countenance, having a mingled air of fun and arrogance. From his Herculean frame, he had received the nickname of "Brom Bones." He was famed for great skill in horsemanship; he was foremost at all races and cockfights; and, with the ascendancy which bodily strength acquires in rustic life, was the umpire in all disputes. He was always ready for either a fight or a frolic, but had more mischief and good humor than ill will in his composition. He had three or four boon companions who regarded him as their model, and at the head of whom he scoured the country, attending every scene of feud or merriment for miles round. Sometimes his crew would be heard dashing along past the farmhouses at midnight, with whoop and halloo, and the old dames would exclaim, "Aye, there goes Brom Bones and his gang!"

This hero had for some time singled out the blooming Katrina for the object of his uncouth gallantries; and though his amorous toyings were something like the gentle caresses of a bear, yet it was whispered that she did not altogether discourage his hopes. Certain it is, his advances were signals for rival candidates to retire; insomuch that, when his horse was seen tied to Van Tassel's paling on a Sunday night, all other suitors passed by in despair.

Such was the formidable rival with whom Ichabod Crane had to contend. Considering all things, a stouter man than he would have shrunk from the competition. Ichabod had, however, a happy mixture of pliability and perseverance in his nature; he was in form and spirit like a supplejack - though he bent, he never broke.

7

To have taken the field openly against his rival would have been madness. Ichabod, therefore, made his advances in a quiet and gently insinuating manner. Under cover of his character of singing master, he had made frequent visits at the farmhouse, carrying on his suit with the daughter by the side of the spring under the great elm, while Balt Van Tassel sat smoking his evening pipe at one end of the piazza and his little wife plied her spinning wheel at the other.

I profess not to know how women's hearts are wooed and won. To me they have always been matters of riddle and admiration. But certain it is that from the moment Ichabod Crane made his advances, the interests of Brom Bones declined; his horse was no longer seen tied at the palings on Sunday nights, and a deadly feud gradually arose between him and the schoolmaster of Sleepy Hollow. Brom would fain have carried matters to open warfare, and Ichabod had overheard a boast by Bones that he would "double the schoolmaster up, and lay him on a shelf of his own schoolhouse"; but Ichabod was too wary to give him an opportunity. Brom had no alternative but to play off boorish practical jokes upon his rival. Bones and his gang of rough riders smoked out Ichabod's singing school by stopping up the chimney; broke into the schoolhouse at night and turned everything topsy-turvy. But what was still more annoying, Brom took opportunities of turning him to ridicule in presence of his mistress, and had a scoundrel dog whom he taught to whine in the most ludicrous manner, and introduced as a rival of Ichabod's to instruct Katrina in psalmody.

In this way matters went on for some time. On a fine autumnal afternoon, Ichabod, in pensive mood, sat enthroned on the lofty stool whence he usually watched all the concerns of his little schoolroom. His scholars were all busily intent upon their books, or slyly whispering behind them with one eye kept upon the master; and a kind of buzzing stillness reigned. It was suddenly interrupted by the appearance of a Negro, mounted on the back of a ragged colt. He came clattering up to the school door with an invitation to Ichabod to attend a merrymaking to be held that evening at Mynheer Van Tassel's.

8

All was now bustle and hubbub in the lately quiet schoolroom. The scholars were hurried through their lessons, without stopping at trifles; those who were tardy had a smart application now and then in the rear to quicken their speed, and the whole school was turned loose an hour before the usual time.

The gallant Ichabod now spent at least an extra half hour at his toilet, brushing and furbishing up his only suit, of rusty black. That he might make his appearance in the true style of a cavalier, he borrowed a horse from the farmer with whom he was staying. The animal was a broken-down plow horse that had outlived almost everything but his viciousness. He was gaunt and shaggy, with a ewe neck and a head like a hammer; his rusty mane and tail were tangled and knotted with burrs; one eye had lost its pupil, and was glaring and spectral, but the other had the gleam of a genuine devil. In his day he must have had fire and mettle, if we may judge from the name he bore of Gunpowder.

Ichabod was a suitable figure for such a steed. He rode with short stirrups, which brought his knees nearly up to the pommel of the saddle; his sharp elbows stuck out like grasshoppers'; he carried his whip perpendicularly in his hand, like a scepter, and, as his horse jogged on, the motion of his arms was not unlike the flapping of a pair of wings. A small wool hat rested nearly on the top of his nose, and the skirts of his black coat fluttered out almost to the horse's tail.

Around him nature wore that rich and golden livery which we always associate with the idea of abundance. As he jogged slowly on his way, his eye ranged with delight over the treasures of jolly autumn. On all sides he beheld vast stores of apples gathered into baskets and barrels for the market, others heaped up in rich piles for the cider press. Farther on he beheld great fields of Indian corn, and the yellow pumpkins lying beneath them, turning up their fair round bellies to the sun. He passed the fragrant buckwheat fields, and as he beheld them, soft anticipations stole over his mind of dainty slapjacks, well buttered and garnished with honey by the delicate little dimpled hand of Katrina Van Tassel. It was toward evening that Ichabod arrived at the castle of the Eleer Van Tassel, which he found thronged with the pride and flower of the adjacent country. Old farmers, a spare leathern-faced race, in homespun coats and breeches, blue stockings, huge shoes, and magnificent pewter buckles. Their brisk withered little dames, in close crimped caps, longwaisted short gowns, homespun petticoats, and gay calico pockets hanging on the outside. Buxom lasses, almost as antiquated in dress as their mothers, excepting where a straw hat, a fine ribbon, or perhaps a white frock gave symptoms of city innovation. The sons, in short square-skirted coats with rows of stupendous brass buttons, and their hair generally queued with an eelskin in the fashion of the times, eelskins being esteemed as a potent nourisher and strengthener of the hair. Brom Bones, however, was the hero of the scene, having come to the gathering on his favorite steed, Daredevil, a creature, like himself, full of mettle and mischief, and which no one but himself could manage.

Brom Bones esquire

9

Ichabod was a kind and thankful creature, whose spirits rose with eating as some men's do with drink. He could not help rolling his large eyes round him on the ample charms of a genuine Dutch country tea table in the sumptuous time of autumn. Such heaped up platters of cakes and crullers[21] of various kinds, known only to experienced Dutch housewives! And then there were apple pies and peach pies and pumpkin pies, besides slices of ham and smoked beef; and, moreover, delectable dishes of preserved plums, and

---

[21] pastries

peaches, and pears, and quinces, not to mention broiled shad and roasted chickens; together with bowls of milk and cream, with the motherly teapot sending up its clouds of vapor from the midst. Ichabod chuckled with the possibility that he might one day be lord of all this scene of almost unimaginable luxury and splendor. Then, he thought, how soon he'd turn his back upon the old schoolhouse and snap his fingers in the face of every niggardly[22] patron!

And now the sound of the music from the hall summoned to the dance. The musician was an old gray-headed Negro, who had been the itinerant orchestra of the neighborhood for more than half a century. His instrument was as old and battered as himself. He accompanied every movement of the bow with a motion of the head, bowing almost to the ground and stamping with his foot whenever a fresh couple were to start.

Ichabod prided himself upon his dancing as much as upon his vocal powers. Not a limb, not a fiber about him was idle as his loosely hung frame in full motion went clattering about the room. How could the flogger of urchins be otherwise than animated and joyous! The lady of his heart was his partner in the dance, and smiling graciously in reply to all his amorous oglings; while Brom Bones, sorely smitten with love and jealousy, sat brooding by himself in one corner.

---

[22] mean

When the dance was at an end, Ichabod was attracted to a knot of the sager folks, who, with old Van Tassel, sat smoking at one end of the piazza, gossiping over former times, and drawing out long stories about ghosts and apparitions, mourning cries and wailings, seen and heard in the neighborhood. Some mention was made of the woman in white, who haunted the dark glen at Raven Rock, and was often heard to shriek on winter nights before a storm, having perished there in the snow. The chief part of the stories, however, turned upon the favorite specter of Sleepy Hollow, the Headless Horseman, who had been heard several times of late near the bridge that crossed the brook in the woody dell next to the church; and, it was said, tethered his horse nightly among the graves in the churchyard.

10

The tale was told of old Brouwer, a most heretical disbeliever in ghosts, how he met the horseman returning from his foray into Sleepy Hollow, and was obliged to get up behind him; how they

galloped over hill and swamp until they reached the church bridge. There the horseman suddenly turned into a skeleton, threw old Brouwer into the brook, and sprang away over the treetops with a clap of thunder.

This story was matched by Brom Bones, who made light of the Galloping Hessian as an arrant [23] jockey. He affirmed that, on returning one night from a neighboring village, he had been overtaken by this midnight trooper; that he had offered to race with him for a bowl of punch, and should have won it, too; but just as they came to the church bridge, the Hessian bolted, and vanished in a flash of fire.

The revel now gradually broke up. The old farmers gathered together their families in their wagons, and were heard for some time rattling along over the distant hills. Some of the damsels mounted behind their favorite swains, and their lighthearted laughter, mingling with the clatter of hoofs, echoed along the silent woodlands. Ichabod only lingered behind, according to the custom of country lovers, to have a tete-a-tete with the heiress, fully

---

[23] complete

convinced that he was now on the highroad to success. Something, however, I fear me, must have gone wrong, for he sallied forth, after no very great interval, with an air quite desolate and chopfallen. Oh, these women! these women! Was Katrina's encouragement of the poor pedagogue[24] all a mere trick to secure her conquest of his rival! Let it suffice to say, Ichabod stole forth with the air of one who had been sacking a henroost, rather than a fair lady's heart. Without looking to the right or left, he went straight to the stable, and with several hearty cuffs and kicks, roused his steed most uncourteously.

It was the very witching time of night that Ichabod, heavyhearted and crestfallen, pursued his travel homeward. Far below, the Tappan Zee spread its dusky waters. In the dead hush of midnight he could hear the faint barking of a watchdog from the opposite shore. The night grew darker and darker; the stars seemed to sink deeper in the sky, and driving clouds occasionally hid them from his sight. He had never felt so lonely and dismal.

11

All the stories of ghosts and goblins that he had heard earlier now came crowding upon his recollection. He would, moreover, soon be approaching the very place where many of the scenes of the ghost stories had been laid.

---

[24] teacher

Just ahead, where a small brook crossed the road, a few rough logs lying side by side served for a bridge. A group of oaks and chestnuts, matted thick with wild grapevines, threw a cavernous gloom over it. Ichabod gave Gunpowder half a score of kicks in his starveling ribs, and attempted to dash briskly across the bridge; but instead of starting forward, the perverse old animal only plunged to the opposite side of the road into a thicket of brambles. He came to a stand just by the bridge, with a suddenness that nearly sent his rider sprawling over his head. Just at this moment, in the dark shadow on the margin of the brook, Ichabod beheld something huge, misshapen, black, and towering. It stirred not, but seemed gathered up in the gloom, like some gigantic monster ready to spring upon the traveler.

The hair of the affrighted schoolteacher rose upon his head, but, summoning up a show of courage, he demanded in stammering accents, "Who are you!" He received no reply. He repeated his demand in a still more agitated voice. Still there was no answer. Once more he cudgeled the sides of the inflexible Gunpowder and, shutting his eyes, broke forth with involuntary fervor into a psalm tune. Just then the shadowy object of alarm put itself in motion and, with a scramble and a bound, stood at once in the middle of the road. He appeared to be a horseman of large dimensions, and mounted on a black horse of powerful frame. He kept aloof on one side of the road, jogging along on the blind side of old Gunpowder, who had now got over his waywardness.

Ichabod quickened his steed, in hopes of leaving this midnight companion behind. The stranger, however, quickened his horse to an equal pace. Ichabod pulled up, and fell into a walk, thinking to lag behind - the other did the same. His heart began to sink within him. There was something in the stranger's moody silence that was appalling. It was soon fearfully accounted for. On mounting a rising ground, which brought the figure of his fellow traveler in relief against the sky, gigantic in height, and muffled in a cloak, Ichabod was horrorstruck on perceiving that he was headless! But his horror was still more increased on observing that the stranger's head was carried before him on the pommel of the saddle.

12

Ichabod's terror rose to desperation; he rained a shower of kicks and blows upon Gunpowder, hoping to give his companion the slip, but the specter started full jump with him. Away then they dashed, stones flying and sparks flashing at every bound. Ichabod's flimsy garments fluttered in the air, as he stretched his long lank body away over his horse's head in the eagerness of his flight.

They had now reached that stretch of the road which descends to Sleepy Hollow, shaded by trees for about a quarter of a mile, where it crosses the famous church bridge just before the green knoll on which stands the church.

Gunpowder, who seemed possessed with a demon, plunged

headlong downhill. As yet his panic had given his unskillful rider an apparent advantage in the chase; but just as he had got halfway through the hollow, the girths of the saddle gave way, and Ichabod felt it slipping from under him. He had just time to save himself by clasping old Gunpowder round the neck when the saddle fell to the earth. He had much ado to maintain his seat, sometimes slipping on one side, sometimes on another, and sometimes jolted on the high ridge of his horse's backbone, with a violence that he feared would cleave him asunder.

An opening in the trees now cheered him with the hopes that the church bridge was at hand. He saw the whitewashed walls of the church dimly glaring under the trees beyond. He recollected the place where Brom Bones's ghostly competitor had disappeared. "If I can but reach that bridge," thought Ichabod, "I am safe." Just then he heard the black steed panting and blowing close behind him; he even fancied that he felt his hot breath. Another convulsive kick in the ribs, and old Gunpowder sprang upon the bridge; he thundered over the resounding planks; he gained the opposite side; and now Ichabod cast a look behind to see if his pursuer should vanish, according to rule, in a flash of fire and brimstone. Just then he saw the goblin rising in his stirrups, in the very act of hurling his head at him. Ichabod endeavored to dodge the horrible missile, but too late. It encountered his cranium with a tremendous crash - he was tumbled headlong into the dust, and Gunpowder, the black steed, and the goblin rider passed by like a whirlwind.

13

The next morning old Gunpowder was found without his saddle, and with the bridle under his feet, soberly cropping the grass at his master's gate. Ichabod did not make his appearance at breakfast; dinner hour came, but no Ichabod. The boys assembled at the schoolhouse, and strolled idly about the banks of the brook; but no schoolmaster. An inquiry was set on foot, and after diligent investigation they came upon the saddle trampled in the dirt. The tracks of horses' hoofs deeply dented in the road were traced to the bridge, beyond which, on the bank of a broad part of the brook, was found the hat of the unfortunate Ichabod, and close beside it a shattered pumpkin. The brook was searched, but the body of the schoolmaster was not to be discovered.

The mysterious event caused much speculation at the church on the following Sunday. Knots of gazers were collected in the churchyard, at the bridge, and at the spot where the hat and pumpkin had been found. They shook their heads, and came to the conclusion that Ichabod had been carried off by the Galloping Hessian. As he was a bachelor, and in nobody's debt, nobody troubled his head anymore about him. It is true, an old farmer who had been down to New York on a visit several years after brought home the intelligence that Ichabod Crane was still alive; that he had only changed his quarters to a distant part of the country, had kept school and studied law at the same time, had turned politician, and finally had been made a justice of the Ten Pound Court. Brom Bones too, who shortly after his rival's disappearance conducted the blooming Katrina to the altar, was observed to look exceedingly knowing whenever the story of Ichabod was related, and always burst into a hearty laugh at the mention of the pumpkin, which led some to suspect that he knew more about the matter than he chose to tell.

The old country wives, however, who are the best judges of these matters, maintain to this day that Ichabod was spirited away by supernatural means. The bridge became more than ever an object of superstitious awe, and that may be the reason why the road has been altered of late years, so as to approach the church by the border of the millpond. The schoolhouse, being deserted, soon fell to decay, and was reported to be haunted by the the ghost of the unfortunate teacher; and the plowboy, loitering homeward of a still summer evening, has often fancied Ichabod's voice at a distance, chanting a melancholy psalm tune among the tranquil solitudes of Sleepy Hollow.

The Tell-Tale Heart

Edgar Allan Poe, 1843

TRUE! --nervous --very, very dreadfully nervous I had been and am; but why will you say that I am mad? The disease had sharpened my senses --not destroyed --not dulled them. Above all was the sense of hearing acute. I heard all things in the heaven and in the earth. I heard many things in hell. How, then, am I mad? Hearken! and observe how healthily --how calmly I can tell you the whole story.

It is impossible to say how first the idea entered my brain; but once conceived, it haunted me day and night. Object there was none. Passion there was none. I loved the old man. He had never wronged me. He had never given me insult. For his gold I had no desire. I think it was his eye! Yes, it was this! He had the eye of a vulture --a pale blue eye, with a film over it. Whenever it fell upon me, my blood ran cold; and so by degrees --very gradually --I made up my mind to take the life of the old man, and thus rid myself of the eye forever.

Now this is the point. You fancy me mad. Madmen know nothing. But you should have seen me. You should have seen how wisely I proceeded --with what caution --with what foresight --with what dissimulation[25] I went to work! I was never kinder to the old man than during the whole week before I killed him. And every night, about midnight, I turned the latch of his door and opened it --oh so gently! And then, when I had made an opening sufficient for my head, I put in a dark lantern, all closed, closed, that no light shone out, and then I thrust in my head. Oh, you would have laughed to see how cunningly I thrust it in! I moved it slowly --very, very slowly, so that I might not disturb the old man's sleep. It took me an hour to place my whole head within the opening so far that I could see him as he lay upon his bed. Ha! would a madman have been so wise as this, And then, when my head was well in the room, I undid the lantern cautiously-oh, so cautiously --cautiously (for the hinges creaked) --I undid it just so much that a single thin ray fell upon the vulture eye. And this I did for seven long nights --every night just at midnight --but I found the eye always closed; and so it was impossible to do the work; for it was not the old man who vexed

---

[25] lying

me, but his Evil Eye. And every morning, when the day broke, I went boldly into the chamber, and spoke courageously to him, calling him by name in a hearty tone, and inquiring how he has passed the night. So you see he would have been a very profound old man, indeed, to suspect that every night, just at twelve, I looked in upon him while he slept.

Upon the eighth night I was more than usually cautious in opening the door. A watch's minute hand moves more quickly than did mine. Never before that night had I felt the extent of my own powers --of my sagacity. [26] I could scarcely contain my feelings of triumph. To think that there I was, opening the door, little by little, and he not even to dream of my secret deeds or thoughts. I fairly chuckled at the idea; and perhaps he heard me; for he moved on the bed suddenly, as if startled. Now you  may think that I drew back --but no. His room was as black as pitch with the thick darkness, (for the shutters were close fastened, through fear of robbers,) and so I knew that he could not see the opening of the door, and I kept pushing it on steadily, steadily.

---

[26] wisdom

I had my head in, and was about to open the lantern, when my thumb slipped upon the tin fastening, and the old man sprang up in bed, crying out --"Who's there?"

I kept quite still and said nothing. For a whole hour I did not move a muscle, and in the meantime I did not hear him lie down. He was still sitting up in the bed listening; --just as I have done, night after night, hearkening to the death watches in the wall.

Presently I heard a slight groan, and I knew it was the groan of mortal terror. It was not a groan of pain or of grief --oh, no! --it was the low stifled sound that arises from the bottom of the soul when overcharged with awe. I knew the sound well. Many a night, just at midnight, when all the world slept, it has welled up from my own bosom, deepening, with its dreadful echo, the terrors that distracted me. I say I knew it well. I knew what the old man felt, and pitied him, although I chuckled at heart. I knew that he had been lying awake ever since the first slight noise, when he had turned in the bed. His fears had been ever since growing upon him. He had been trying to fancy them causeless, but could not. He had been saying to himself --"It is nothing but the wind in the chimney --it is only a mouse crossing the floor," or "It is merely a cricket which has made a single chirp." Yes, he had been trying to comfort himself with these suppositions: but he had found all in vain. All in vain; because Death, in approaching him had stalked with his black shadow before him, and enveloped the victim. And it was the mournful influence of the unperceived shadow that caused him to feel --although he neither saw nor heard --to feel the presence of my head within the room.

When I had waited a long time, very patiently, without hearing him lie down, I resolved to open a little --a very, very little crevice in the lantern. So I opened it --you cannot imagine how stealthily, stealthily --until, at length a simple dim ray, like the thread of the spider, shot from out the crevice and fell full upon the vulture eye. It was open -- wide, wide open --and I grew furious as I gazed upon it. I saw it with perfect distinctness --all a dull blue, with a hideous veil over it that chilled the very marrow in my bones; but I could see nothing else of the old man's face or person: for I had directed the ray as if by instinct, precisely upon the damned spot.

And have I not told you that what you mistake for madness is but over-acuteness of the sense? --now, I say, there came to my ears a low, dull, quick sound, such as a watch makes when enveloped in cotton. I knew that sound well, too. It was the beating of the old man's heart. It increased my fury, as the beating of a drum stimulates the soldier into courage.

But even yet I refrained and kept still. I scarcely breathed. I held the lantern motionless. I tried how steadily I could maintain the ray upon the eve. Meantime the hellish tattoo of the heart increased. It grew quicker and quicker, and louder and louder every instant. The old man's terror must have been extreme! It grew louder, I say, louder every moment! --do you mark me well I have told you that I am nervous: so I am. And now at the dead hour of the night, amid the dreadful silence of that old house, so strange a noise as this excited me to uncontrollable terror. Yet, for some minutes longer I refrained and stood still. But the beating grew louder, louder! I thought the heart must burst. And now a new anxiety seized me --the sound would be heard by a neighbour! The old man's hour had come! With a loud yell, I threw open the lantern and leaped into the room. He shrieked once --once only. In an instant I dragged him to the floor, and pulled the heavy bed over him. I then smiled gaily, to find the deed so far done. But, for many minutes, the heart beat on with a muffled sound. This, however, did not vex me; it would not be heard through the wall. At length it ceased. The old man was dead. I removed the bed and examined the corpse. Yes, he was stone, stone dead. I placed my hand upon the heart and held it there many minutes. There was no pulsation. He was stone dead. His eve would trouble me no more.

If still you think me mad, you will think so no longer when I describe the wise precautions I took for the concealment of the body. The night waned, and I worked hastily, but in silence. First of all I dismembered the corpse. I cut off the head and the arms and the legs.

I then took up three planks from the flooring of the chamber, and deposited all between the scantlings. I then replaced the boards so cleverly, so cunningly, that no human eye --not even his --could have detected any thing wrong. There was nothing to wash out --no stain of any kind --no blood-spot whatever. I had been too wary for that. A tub had caught all --ha! ha!

When I had made an end of these labors, it was four o'clock --still dark as midnight. As the bell sounded the hour, there came a knocking at the street door. I went down to open it with a light heart, --for what had I now to fear? There entered three men, who introduced themselves, with perfect suavity[27], as officers of the police. A shriek had been heard by a neighbour during the night; suspicion of foul play had been aroused; information had been lodged at the police office, and they (the officers) had been deputed to search the premises.

I smiled, --for what had I to fear? I bade the gentlemen welcome. The shriek, I said, was my own in a dream. The old man, I mentioned, was absent in the country. I took my visitors all over the house. I bade them search --search well. I led them, at length, to his chamber. I showed them his treasures, secure, undisturbed. In the enthusiasm of my confidence, I brought chairs into the room, and desired them here to rest from their fatigues, while I myself, in the wild audacity[28] of my perfect triumph, placed my own seat upon the very spot beneath which reposed the corpse of the victim.

---

[27] sophistication
[28] daring

The officers were satisfied. My manner had convinced them. I was

 singularly at ease. They sat, and while I answered cheerily, they chatted of familiar things. But, ere long, I felt myself getting pale and wished them gone. My head ached, and I fancied a ringing in my ears: but still they sat and still chatted. The ringing became more distinct: --It continued and became more distinct: I talked more freely to get rid of the feeling: but it continued and gained definiteness --until, at length, I found that the noise was not within my ears.

No doubt I now grew very pale; --but I talked more fluently, and with a heightened voice. Yet the sound increased --and what could I do? It was a low, dull, quick sound --much such a sound as a watch makes when enveloped in cotton. I gasped for breath --and yet the officers heard it not. I talked more quickly --more vehemently; but the noise steadily increased. I arose and argued about trifles, in a high key and with violent gesticulations; but the noise steadily increased. Why would they not be gone? I paced the floor to and fro with heavy strides, as if excited to fury by the observations of the men --but the noise steadily increased. Oh God! what could I do? I foamed --I raved --I swore! I swung the chair upon which I had been sitting, and grated it upon the boards, but the noise arose over all and continually increased. It grew louder --louder --louder! And still the men chatted pleasantly, and smiled. Was it possible they heard not? Almighty God! --no, no! They heard! --they suspected! --they knew! --they were making a mockery of my horror!-this I thought, and this I think. But anything was better than this agony! Anything was more tolerable than this derision! I could bear those hypocritical smiles no longer! I felt that I must scream or die! and now --again! --hark! louder! louder! louder! louder!

"Villains!" I shrieked, "dissemble no more! I admit the deed! --tear up the planks! here, here! --It is the beating of his hideous heart!"

The Very Selfish Giant

Oscar Wilde, 1888

Every afternoon, as they were coming from school, the children used to go and play in the Giant's garden. It was a large lovely garden, with soft green grass. Here and there over the grass stood beautiful flowers like stars, and there were twelve peach-trees that in the spring-time broke out into delicate blossoms of pink and pearl, and in the autumn bore rich fruit. The birds sat on the trees and sang so sweetly that the children used to stop their games in order to listen to them. 'How happy we are here!' they cried to each other.

One day the Giant came back. He had been to visit his friend the Cornish ogre, and had stayed with him for seven years. After the seven years were over he had said all that he had to say, for his conversation was limited, and he determined to return to his own castle. When he arrived he saw the children playing in the garden.

'What are you doing here?' he cried in a very gruff voice, and the children ran away. 'My own garden is my own garden,' said the Giant; 'any one can understand that, and I will allow nobody to play in it but myself.' So he built a high wall all round it, and put up a notice-board.

TRESPASSERS

WILL BE

PROSECUTED

He was a very selfish Giant.

The poor children had now nowhere to play. They tried to play on the road, but the road was very dusty and full of hard stones, and they did not like it. They used to wander round the high wall when their lessons were over, and talk about the beautiful garden inside. 'How happy we were there,' they said to each other.

Then the Spring came, and all over the country there were little blossoms and little birds. Only in the garden of the Selfish Giant it was still Winter. The birds did not care to sing in it as there were no children, and the trees forgot to blossom. Once a beautiful flower put its head out from the grass, but when it saw the notice-board it was so sorry for the children that it slipped back into the ground again, and went off to sleep. The only people who were pleased were the Snow and the Frost. 'Spring has forgotten this garden,' they cried, 'so we will live here all the year round.' The Snow covered up the grass with her great white cloak, and the Frost painted all the trees silver. Then they invited the North Wind to stay with them, and he came. He was wrapped in furs, and he roared all day about the garden, and blew the chimney-pots down. 'This is a delightful spot,' he said, 'we must ask the Hail on a visit.' So the Hail came. Every day for three hours he rattled on the roof of the castle till he broke most of the slates, and then he ran round and round the garden as fast as he could go. He was dressed in grey, and his breath was like ice.

'I cannot understand why the Spring is so late in coming,' said the Selfish Giant, as he sat at the window and looked out at his cold white garden; 'I hope there will be a change in the weather.'

But the Spring never came, nor the Summer. The Autumn gave golden fruit to every garden, but to the Giant's garden she gave none. 'He is too selfish,' she said. So it was always Winter there, and the North Wind, and the Hail, and the Frost, and the Snow danced about through the trees.

One morning the Giant was lying awake in bed when he heard some lovely music. It sounded so sweet to his ears that he thought it must be the King's musicians passing by. It was really only a little linnet singing outside his window, but it was so long since he had heard a bird sing in his garden that it seemed to him to be the most beautiful music in the world. Then the Hail stopped dancing over his head, and the North Wind ceased roaring, and a delicious perfume came to him through the open casement. 'I believe the Spring has come at last,' said the Giant; and he jumped out of bed and looked out. What did he see? He saw a most wonderful sight.

Through a little hole in the wall the children had crept in, and they were sitting in the branches of the trees. In every tree that he could see there was a little child. And the trees were so glad to have the children back again that they had covered themselves with blossoms, and were waving their arms gently above the children's heads. The birds were flying about and twittering with delight, and the flowers were looking up through the green grass and laughing. It was a lovely scene, only in one corner it was still Winter. It was the farthest corner of the garden, and in it was standing a little boy. He was so small that he could not reach up to the branches of the tree, and he was wandering all round it, crying bitterly. The poor tree was still quite covered with frost and snow, and the North Wind was blowing and roaring above it. 'Climb up! little boy,' said the Tree, and it bent its branches down as low as it could; but the little boy was too tiny.

And the Giant's heart melted as he looked out. 'How selfish I have been!' he said. 'Now I know why the Spring would not come here. I will put that poor little boy on the top of the tree, and then I will knock down the wall, and my garden shall be the children's playground for ever and ever.' He was really very sorry for what he had done.

So he crept downstairs and opened the front door quite softly, and went out into the garden. But when the children saw him they were so frightened that they all ran away, and the garden became Winter again. Only the little boy did not run, for his eyes were so full of tears that he did not see the Giant coming. And the Giant stole up behind him and took him gently in his hand, and put him up into the tree. And the tree broke at once into blossom, and the birds came and sang on it, and the little boy stretched out his two arms and flung them round the Giant's neck, and kissed him. And the other children, when they saw that the Giant was not wicked any longer, came running back, and with them came the Spring. 'It is your garden now, little children,' said the Giant, and he took a great axe and knocked down the wall. And when the people were gong to market at twelve o'clock they found the Giant playing with the children in the most beautiful garden they had ever seen.

All day long they played, and in the evening they came to the Giant to bid him good-bye. 'But where is your little companion?' he said: 'the boy I put into the tree.' The Giant loved him the best because he had kissed him.

'We don't know,' answered the children; 'he has gone away.'

'You must tell him to be sure and come here to-morrow,' said the Giant. But the children said that they did not know where he lived, and had never seen him before; and the Giant felt very sad.

Every afternoon, when school was over, the children came and played with the Giant. But the little boy whom the Giant loved was never seen again. The Giant was very kind to all the children, yet he longed for his first little friend, and often spoke of him. 'How I would like to see him!' he used to say.

Years went over, and the Giant grew very old and feeble. He could not play about any more, so he sat in a huge armchair, and watched the children at their games, and admired his garden. 'I have many beautiful flowers,' he said; 'but the children are the most beautiful flowers of all.'

One winter morning he looked out of his window as he was dressing. He did not hate the Winter now, for he knew that it was merely the Spring asleep, and that the flowers were resting. Suddenly he rubbed his eyes in wonder, and looked and looked. It certainly was a marvellous sight. In the farthest corner of the garden was a tree quite covered with lovely white blossoms. Its branches were all golden, and silver fruit hung down from them, and underneath it stood the little boy he had loved.

Downstairs ran the Giant in great joy, and out into the garden. He hastened across the grass, and came near to the child. And when he came quite close his face grew red with anger, and he said, 'Who hath dared to wound thee?' For on the palms of the child's hands were the prints of two nails, and the prints of two nails were on the little feet.

'Who hath dared to wound thee?' cried the Giant; 'tell me, that I may take my big sword and slay him.'

'Nay!' answered the child; 'but these are the wounds of Love.'

'Who art thou?' said the Giant, and a strange awe fell on him, and he knelt before the little child.

And the child smiled on the Giant, and said to him, 'You let me play once in your garden, to-day you shall come with me to my garden, which is Paradise.' And when the children ran in that afternoon, they found the Giant lying dead under the tree, all covered with white blossoms.

Blue Beard

Charles Perrault, 1895

Once on a time there was a man who had fine town and country houses, gold and silver plate, embroidered furniture, and coaches gilt all over; but unfortunately, this man had a blue beard, which made him look so ugly and terrible, that there was not a woman or girl who did not run away from him. One of his neighbours, a lady of quality, had two daughters, who were perfectly beautiful. He proposed to marry one of them, leaving her to choose which of the two she would give him. Neither of them would have him; and they sent him from one to the other, not being able to make up their minds to marry a man who had a blue beard. What increased their distaste to him was, that he had had several wives already, and nobody knew what had become of them.

Blue Beard, in order to cultivate their acquaintance[29], took them, with their mother, three or four of their most intimate friends, and some young persons who resided in the neighbourhood, to one of his country seats, where they passed an entire week. Nothing was thought of but excursions, hunting and fishing, parties, balls, entertainments, collations[30]; nobody went to bed; the whole night was spent in merry games and gambols. In short, all went off so well, that the youngest daughter began to find out that the beard of the master of the house was not as blue as it used to be, and that he was a very worthy man. Immediately upon their return to town the marriage took place.

At the end of a month Blue Beard told his wife that he was obliged to take a journey, which would occupy six weeks at least, on a matter of great consequence; that he entreated she would amuse herself as much as she could during his absence; that she would invite her best friends, take them into the country with her if she pleased, and keep an excellent table everywhere. "Here," said he to her, "are the keys of my two great store-rooms;

---

[29] get to know them
[30] informal meals

these are those of the chests in which the gold and silver plate is kept, that is only used on particular occasions; these are the keys of

 the strong boxes in which I keep my money; these open the caskets that contain my jewels; and this is the pass-key of all the apartments. As for this little key, it is that of the closet at the end of the long gallery, on the ground floor. Open everything, and go everywhere except into that little closet, which I forbid you to enter, and I forbid you so strictly, that if you should venture to open the door, there is nothing that you may not have to dread from my anger!"

She promised to observe implicitly all his directions, and after he had embraced her, he got on to his horse and set out on his journey.

The neighbours and friends of the young bride did not wait for her invitation, so eager were they to see all the treasures contained in the mansion, not having ventured to enter it while the husband was at home, so terrified were they at his blue beard. Behold them immediately running through all the rooms, closets, and wardrobes, each apartment exceeding the other in beauty and richness. They ascended afterwards to the store-rooms, where they could not sufficiently admire the number and elegance of the tapestries, the beds, the sofas, the cabinets, the stands, the tables, and the mirrors in which they could see themselves from head to foot, and that had frames some of glass, some of silver, and some of gilt metal, more beautiful and magnificent than had ever been seen.

They never ceased enlarging upon and envying the good fortune of their friend, who in the meanwhile was not in the least entertained by the sight of all these treasures, in consequence of her impatience to open the closet on the ground floor. Her curiosity increased to such a degree that, without reflecting how rude it was to leave her company, she ran down a back staircase in such haste that twice or thrice she narrowly escaped breaking her neck.

Arrived at the door of the closet, she paused for a moment, bethinking herself of her husband's prohibition, and that some misfortune might befall her for her  disobedience; but the temptation was so strong that she could not conquer it. She therefore took the little key and opened, tremblingly, the door of the closet. At first she could discern nothing, the windows being closed; after a short time she began to perceive that the floor was all covered with clotted blood, in which were reflected the dead bodies of several females suspended against the walls. These were all the wives of Blue Beard, who had cut their throats one after the other.

She was ready to die with fright, and the key of the closet, which she had withdrawn from the lock, fell from her hand.

After recovering her senses a little, she picked up the key, locked the door again, and went up to her chamber to compose herself; but she could not succeed, so greatly was she agitated. Having observed that the key of the closet was stained with blood, she wiped it two or three times, but the blood would not come off. In vain she washed it, and even scrubbed it with sand and freestone, the blood was still there, for the key was enchanted, and there were no means of cleaning it completely: when the blood was washed off one side, it came back on the other.

Blue Beard returned that very evening, and said that he had received letters on the road informing him that the business on which he was going had been settled to his advantage. His wife did all she could to persuade him that she was delighted at his speedy return.

The next morning he asked her for his keys again; she gave them to him; but her hand trembled so, that he had not much difficulty in guessing what had occurred. "How comes it," said he, "that the key of the closet is not with the others?"

"I must have left it," she replied, "up-stairs on my table."

"Fail not," said Blue Beard, "to give it me presently."

After several excuses, she was compelled to produce the key. Blue Beard having examined it, said to his wife, "Why is there some blood on this key?"

"I don't know," answered the poor wife, paler than death.

"You don't know?" rejoined Blue Beard. "I know well enough. You must needs enter the closet. Well, madam, you shall enter it, and go take your place amongst the ladies you saw there." She flung herself at her husband's feet, weeping and begging his pardon, with all the signs of true repentance for having disobeyed him. Her beauty and affliction might have melted a rock, but Blue Beard had a heart harder than a rock. "You must die, madam," said he, "and immediately."

"If I must die," she replied, looking at him with streaming eyes, "give me a little time to say my prayers."

"I give you half a quarter of an hour," answered Blue Beard, "but not a minute more."

As soon as he had left her, she called her sister, and said to her, "Sister Anne" (for so she was named), "go up, I pray thee, to the top of the tower, and see if my brothers are not coming. They have promised me that they would come to see me today; and if you see them, sign to them to make haste." Sister Anne mounted to the top of the tower, and the poor distressed creature called to her every now and then, "Anne! Sister Anne! Dost thou not see anything coming?"

And sister Anne answered her, "I see nothing but the sun making dust, and the grass growing green."

In the meanwhile Blue Beard, with a great cutlass in his hand, called out with all his might to his wife, "Come down quickly, or I will come up there."

"One minute more, if you please," replied his wife; and immediately repeated in a low voice, "Anne! Sister Anne! Dost thou not see anything coming?"

And sister Anne replied, "I see nothing but the sun making dust, and the grass growing green."

"Come down quickly," roared Blue Beard, "or I will come up there."

"I come," answered his wife, and then exclaimed, "Anne! Sister Anne! Dost thou not see anything coming?"

"I see," said sister Anne, "a great cloud of dust moving this way." "Is it my brothers?" "Alas! no, sister, I see a flock of sheep."

"Wilt thou not come down?" shouted Blue Beard.

"One minute more," replied his wife, and then she cried, "Anne! Sister Anne! Dost thou not see anything coming?"

"I see," she replied, "two horsemen coming this way; but they are still at a great distance."

"Heaven be praised!" she exclaimed, a moment afterwards. "They are my brothers! I am making all the signs I can to hasten them."

Blue Beard began to roar so loudly that the whole house shook again. The poor wife descended, and went and threw herself, with streaming eyes and dishevelled tresses, at his feet. "It is of no use," said Blue Beard. "You must die!" Then seizing her by the hair with one hand, and raising his cutlass with the other, he was about to cut off her head. The poor wife turned towards him, and fixing upon him her dying eyes, implored him to allow her one short moment to collect herself. "No, no," said he; "recommend thyself heartily to Heaven." And lifting his arm——

At this moment there was so loud a knocking at the gate, that Blue Beard stopped short. It was opened, and two horsemen were

immediately seen to enter, who, drawing their swords, ran straight at Blue Beard. He recognized them as the brothers of his wife— one a dragoon [31], the other a musqueteer, and, consequently, fled immediately, in hope to escape; but they pursued him so closely, that they overtook him before he could reach the step of his door, and, passing their swords through his body, left him dead

---

[31] cavalry soldier

on the spot. The poor wife was almost as dead as her husband, and had not strength to rise and embrace her brothers.

It was found that Blue Beard had no heirs, and so his widow remained possessed of all his property. She employed part of it in marrying her sister Anne to a young gentleman who had long loved her; another part, in buying captains' commissions for her two brothers, and with the rest she married herself to a very worthy man, who made her forget the miserable time she had passed with Blue Beard.

The Monkey's Paw

W.W. Jacobs, 1906

I

Without, the night was cold and wet, but in the small parlour of Laburnam Villa the blinds were drawn and the fire burned brightly. Father and son were at chess, the former, who possessed ideas about the game, involving radical changes, put his king into such sharp and unnecessary perils that it even provoked comment from the white-haired old lady knitting placidly by the fire.

'Hark at the wind,' said Mr. White, who, having seen a fatal mistake after it was too late, was amiably[32] desirous of preventing his son from seeing it.

'I'm listening," said the latter, grimly surveying the board as he stretched out his hand. 'Check.'

'I should hardly think that he'd come to-night,' said his father, with his hand poised over the board.

---

[32] in a friendly manner

'Mate,' replied the son.

'That's the worst of living so far out,' bawled Mr. White, with sudden and unlooked-for violence; 'of all the beastly, slushy, out-of-the-way places to live in, this is the worst. Pathway's a bog, and the road's a torrent. I don't know what people are thinking about. I suppose because only two houses on the road are let, they think it doesn't matter.'

'Never mind, dear,' said his wife soothingly; 'perhaps you'll win the next one.'

Mr. White looked up sharply, just in time to intercept a knowing glance between mother and son. The words died away on his lips, and he hid a guilty grin in his thin grey beard.

'There he is,' said Herbert White, as the gate banged to loudly and heavy footsteps came toward the door. The old man rose with hospitable haste, and opening the door, was heard condoling[33] with the new arrival. The new arrival also condoled with himself, so that Mrs. White said, 'Tut, tut!' and coughed gently as her husband entered the room, followed by a tall burly man, beady of eye and

---

[33] sympathising

rubicund of visage[34]. 'Sergeant-Major Morris,' he said, introducing him.

The sergeant-major shook hands, and taking the proffered seat by the fire, watched contentedly while his host got out whisky and tumblers and stood a small copper kettle on the fire. At the third glass his eyes got brighter, and he began to talk, the little family circle regarding with eager interest this visitor from distant parts, as he squared his broad shoulders in the chair and spoke of strange scenes and doughty deeds; of wars and plagues and strange peoples.

'Twenty-one years of it,' said Mr. White, nodding at his wife and son. 'When he went away he was a slip of a youth in the warehouse. Now look at him.'

'He don't look to have taken much harm,' said Mrs. White, politely.

'I'd like to go to India myself,' said the old man, 'just to look round a bit, you know.'

'Better where you are,' said the sergeant-major, shaking his head. He put down the empty glass, and sighing softly, shook it again.

---

[34] rosy cheeked

'I should like to see those old temples and fakirs and jugglers,' said the old man. 'What was that you started telling me the other day about a monkey's paw or something, Morris?'

'Nothing,' said the soldier hastily. 'Leastways, nothing worth hearing.'

'Monkey's paw?' said Mrs. White curiously.

'Well, it's just a bit of what you might call magic, perhaps,' said the sergeant-major off-handedly. His three listeners leaned forward eagerly. The visitor absentmindedly put his empty glass to his lips and then set it down again. His host filled it for him. 'To look at,' said the sergeant-major, fumbling in his pocket, 'it's just an ordinary little paw, dried to a mummy.' He took something out of his pocket and proffered it. Mrs. White drew back with a grimace, but her son, taking it, examined it curiously.

'And what is there special about it?' inquired Mr. White, as he took it from his son and, having examined it, placed it upon the table. 'It had a spell put on it by an old fakir,' said the sergeant-major, 'a very holy man. He wanted to show that fate ruled people's lives, and  that those who interfered with it did so to their sorrow. He put a spell on it so that three separate men could each have three wishes from it.'

His manner was so impressive that his hearers were conscious that their light laughter jarred somewhat. 'Well, why don't you have three, sir?' said Herbert White cleverly.

The soldier regarded him in the way that middle age is wont to regard presumptuous youth. 'I have,' he said quietly, and his blotchy face whitened.

'And did you really have the three wishes granted?' asked Mrs. White.

'I did,' said the sergeant-major, and his glass tapped against his strong teeth.

'And has anybody else wished?' inquired the old lady.

'The first man had his three wishes, yes,' was the reply. 'I don't know what the first two were, but the third was for death. That's how I got the paw.' His tones were so grave that a hush fell upon the group.

'If you've had your three wishes, it's no good to you now, then, Morris,' said the old man at last. 'What do you keep it for?'

The soldier shook his head. 'Fancy, I suppose,' he said slowly.

'If you could have another three wishes,' said the old man, eyeing him keenly, 'would you have them?'

'I don't know,' said the other. 'I don't know.'

He took the paw, and dangling it between his front finger and thumb, suddenly threw it upon the fire. White, with a slight cry, stooped down and snatched it off. 'Better let it burn,' said the soldier solemnly.

'If you don't want it, Morris,' said the old man, 'give it to me.'

'I won't,' said his friend doggedly. 'I threw it on the fire. If you keep it, don't blame me for what happens. Pitch it on the fire again, like a sensible man.'

The other shook his head and examined his new possession closely. 'How do you do it?' he inquired.

'Hold it up in your right hand and wish aloud,' said the sergeant-major, 'but I warn you of the consequences.'

'Sounds like the Arabian Nights,' said Mrs White, as she rose and began to set the supper. 'Don't you think you might wish for four pairs of hands for me?' Her husband drew the talisman from his pocket and then all three burst into laughter as the sergeant-major, with a look of alarm on his face, caught him by the arm.

'If you must wish,' he said gruffly, 'wish for something sensible.'

Mr. White dropped it back into his pocket, and placing chairs, motioned his friend to the table. In the business of supper the talisman was partly forgotten, and afterward the three sat listening in an enthralled fashion to a second instalment of the soldier's adventures in India.

'If the tale about the monkey paw is not more truthful than those he has been telling us,' said Herbert, as the door closed behind their guest, just in time for him to catch the last train, 'we shan't make much out of it.'

'Did you give him anything for it, father?' inquired Mrs. White, regarding her husband closely.

'A trifle,' said he, colouring slightly. 'He didn't want it, but I made him take it. And he pressed me again to throw it away.'

'Likely,' said Herbert, with pretended horror. 'Why, we're going to be rich, and famous, and happy. Wish to be an emperor, father, to begin with; then you can't be henpecked.' He darted round the table, pursued by the maligned Mrs. White armed with an antimacassar[35].

Mr. White took the paw from his pocket and eyed it dubiously. I don't know what to wish for, and that's a fact,' he said slowly. 'It seems to me I've got all I want.'

'If you only cleared the house, you'd be quite happy, wouldn't you?' said Herbert, with his hand on his shoulder. 'Well, wish for two

---

[35] a small piece of cloth placed over furniture

hundred pounds, then; that'll just do it.'

His father, smiling shamefacedly at his own credulity, held up the talisman, as his son, with a solemn face somewhat marred by a wink at his mother, sat down at the piano and struck a few impressive chords. 'I wish for two hundred pounds,' said the old man distinctly.

A fine crash from the piano greeted the words, interrupted by a shuddering cry from the old man. His wife and son ran toward him. 'It moved,' he cried, with a glance of disgust at the object as it lay on the floor. 'As I wished, it twisted in my hands like a snake.'

'Well, I don't see the money,' said his son, as he picked it up and placed it on the table, 'and I bet I never shall.'

'It must have been your fancy, father,' said his wife, regarding him anxiously.

He shook his head. 'Never mind, though; there's no harm done, but it gave me a shock all the same.'

They sat down by the fire again while the two men finished their pipes. Outside, the wind was higher than ever, and the old man started nervously at the sound of a door banging upstairs. A silence unusual and depressing settled upon all three, which lasted until the old couple rose to retire for the night.

'I expect you'll find the cash tied up in a big bag in the middle of your bed,' said Herbert, as he bade them good-night, 'and something horrible squatting up on top of the wardrobe watching you as you pocket your ill-gotten gains.' He sat alone in the darkness, gazing at the dying fire, and seeing faces in it. The last face was so horrible and so simian [36] that he gazed at it in amazement. It got so vivid that, with a little uneasy laugh, he felt on the table for a glass containing a little water to throw over it. His hand grasped the monkey's paw, and with a little shiver he wiped his hand on his coat and went up to bed.

II

In the brightness of the wintry sun next morning as it streamed over the breakfast table Herbert laughed at his fears. There was an air of prosaic[37] wholesomeness about the room that it had lacked on the previous night, and the dirty, shrivelled little paw was pitched on the

---

[36] ape-like
[37] ordinary

sideboard with a carelessness which betokened no great belief in its virtues.

'I suppose all old soldiers are the same,' said Mrs White. 'The idea of our listening to such nonsense! How could wishes be granted in these days? And if they could, how could two hundred pounds hurt you, father?'

'Might drop on his head from the sky,' said the frivolous Herbert.

'Morris said the things happened so naturally,' said his father, 'that you might if you so wished attribute it to coincidence.'

'Well, don't break into the money before I come back,' said Herbert, as he rose from the table. 'I'm afraid it'll turn you into a mean, avaricious man, and we shall have to disown you.'

His mother laughed, and following him to the door, watched him down the road, and returning to the breakfast table, was very happy at the expense of her husband's credulity[38]. All of which did not prevent her from scurrying to the door at the postman's knock, nor prevent her from referring somewhat shortly to retired sergeant-

---

[38] accepting without question

majors of bibulous habits[39] when she found that the post brought a tailor's bill.

'Herbert will have some more of his funny remarks, I expect, when he comes home,' she said, as they sat at dinner.

'I dare say,' said Mr. White, pouring himself out some beer; 'but for all that, the thing moved in my hand; that I'll swear to.'

'You thought it did,' said the old lady soothingly.

'I say it did,' replied the other. 'There was no thought about it; I had just----What's the matter?'

His wife made no reply. She was watching the mysterious movements of a man outside, who, peering in an undecided fashion at the house, appeared to be trying to make up his mind to enter. In mental connection with the two hundred pounds, she noticed that the stranger was well dressed and wore a silk hat of glossy newness. Three times he paused at the gate, and then walked on again. The fourth time he stood with his hand upon it, and then with sudden resolution flung it open and walked up the path. Mrs. White at the same moment placed her hands behind her, and hurriedly

---

[39] fondness for alcohol

unfastening the strings of her apron, put that useful article of apparel beneath the cushion of her chair.

She brought the stranger, who seemed ill at ease, into the room. He gazed at her furtively, and listened in a preoccupied fashion as the old lady apologized for the appearance of the room, and her husband's coat, a garment which he usually reserved for the garden. She then waited as patiently as her sex would permit, for him to broach his business, but he was at first strangely silent.

'I was asked to call,' he said at last, and stooped and picked a piece of cotton from his trousers. 'I come from Maw and Meggins.'

The old lady started. 'Is anything the matter?' she asked breathlessly. 'Has anything happened to Herbert? What is it? What is it?'

Her husband interposed. 'There, there, mother,' he said hastily. 'Sit down, and don't jump to conclusions. You've not brought bad news, I'm sure, sir,' and he eyed the other wistfully.

'I'm sorry---- ' began the visitor.

'Is he hurt?' demanded the mother.

The visitor bowed in assent. 'Badly hurt,' he said quietly, 'but he is not in any pain.'

'Oh, thank God!' said the old woman, clasping her hands. 'Thank God for that! Thank ---' She broke off suddenly as the sinister meaning of the assurance dawned upon her and she saw the awful confirmation of her fears in the other's averted face. She caught her breath, and turning to her slower-witted husband, laid her trembling old hand upon his. There was a long silence.

'He was caught in the machinery,' said the visitor at length, in a low voice.

'Caught in the machinery,' repeated Mr. White, in a dazed fashion, 'yes.' He sat staring blankly out at the window, and taking his wife's hand between his own, pressed it as he had been wont to do in their old courting days nearly forty years before. 'He was the only one left to us,' he said, turning gently to the visitor. 'It is hard.'

The other coughed, and rising, walked slowly to the window. 'The firm wished me to convey their sincere sympathy with you in your great loss,' he said, without looking round. 'I beg that you will understand I am only their servant and merely obeying orders.'

There was no reply; the old woman's face was white, her eyes staring, and her breath inaudible; on the husband's face was a look such as his friend the sergeant might have carried into his first action.

'I was to say that Maw and Meggins disclaim all responsibility,' continued the other. 'They admit no liability at all, but in consideration of your son's services they wish to present you with a certain sum as compensation.'

Mr. White dropped his wife's hand, and rising to his feet, gazed with a look of horror at his visitor. His dry lips shaped the words, 'How much?'

'Two hundred pounds,' was the answer.

Unconscious of his wife's shriek, the old man smiled faintly, put out his hands like a sightless man, and dropped, a senseless heap, to the floor.

III

In the huge new cemetery, some two miles distant, the old people buried their dead, and came back to a house steeped in shadow and silence. It was all over so quickly that at first they could hardly realize it, and remained in a state of expectation as though of something else to happen--something else which was to lighten this load, too heavy for old hearts to bear. But the days passed, and expectation gave place to resignation--the hopeless resignation of the old, sometimes miscalled, apathy. Sometimes they hardly exchanged a word, for now they had nothing to talk about, and their days were long to weariness.

It was about a week after that that the old man, waking suddenly in the night, stretched out his hand and found himself alone. The room was in darkness, and the sound of subdued weeping came from the window. He raised himself in bed and listened.

'Come back,' he said tenderly. 'You will be cold.'

'It is colder for my son,' said the old woman, and wept afresh. The sound of her sobs died away on his ears. The bed was warm, and his eyes heavy with sleep. He dozed fitfully, and then slept until a sudden wild cry from his wife awoke him with a start.

'The paw!' she cried wildly. 'The monkey's paw!'

He started up in alarm. 'Where? Where is it? What's the matter?'

She came stumbling across the room toward him. 'I want it,' she said quietly. 'You've not destroyed it?'

'It's in the parlour, on the bracket,' he replied, marvelling. 'Why?'
She cried and laughed together, and bending over, kissed his cheek. 'I only just thought of it,' she said hysterically. 'Why didn't I think of it before? Why didn't you think of it?'

'Think of what?' he questioned.

'The other two wishes,' she replied rapidly. 'We've only had one.'

'Was not that enough?' he demanded fiercely.

'No,' she cried, triumphantly; 'we'll have one more. Go down and get it quickly, and wish our boy alive again.'

The man sat up in bed and flung the bedclothes from his quaking limbs. 'Good God, you are mad!' he cried aghast.

'Get it,' she panted; 'get it quickly, and wish----Oh, my boy, my boy!'

Her husband struck a match and lit the candle. 'Get back to bed,' he said, unsteadily. 'You don't know what you are saying.'

'We had the first wish granted,' said the old woman, feverishly; 'why not the second.'

'A coincidence,' stammered the old man.

'Go and get it and wish,' cried the old woman, quivering with excitement.

The old man turned and regarded her, and his voice shook. 'He has been dead ten days, and besides he--I would not tell you else, but--I could only recognize him by his clothing. If he was too terrible for you to see then, how now?'

'Bring him back,' cried the old woman, and dragged him toward the door. 'Do you think I fear the child I have nursed?'

He went down in the darkness, and felt his way to the parlour, and then to the mantelpiece. The talisman was in its place, and a horrible fear that the unspoken wish might bring his mutilated son before him ere he could escape from the room seized upon him, and he caught his breath as he found that he had lost the direction of the door. His brow cold with sweat, he felt his way round the table, and groped along the wall until he found himself in the small passage with the unwholesome thing in his hand. Even his wife's face seemed changed as he entered the room. It was white and expectant, and to his fears seemed to have an unnatural look upon it. He was afraid of her.

'Wish!' she cried, in a strong voice.

'It is foolish and wicked,' he faltered.

'Wish!' repeated his wife.

He raised his hand. 'I wish my son alive again.'

The talisman fell to the floor, and he regarded it fearfully. Then he sank trembling into a chair as the old woman, with burning eyes, walked to the window and raised the blind. He sat until he was chilled with the cold, glancing occasionally at the figure of the old woman peering through the window. The candle end, which had burnt below the rim of the china candlestick, was throwing pulsating shadows on the ceiling and walls, until, with a flicker larger than the rest, it expired. The old man, with an unspeakable sense of relief at the failure of the talisman, crept back to his bed, and a minute or two afterward the old woman came silently and apathetically [40] beside him. Neither spoke, but both lay silently listening to the

---

[40] lazily, without energy

ticking of the clock. A stair creaked, and a squeaky mouse scurried noisily through the wall.

The darkness was oppressive, and after lying for some time screwing up his courage, the husband took the box of matches, and striking one, went downstairs for a candle. At the foot of the stairs the match went out, and he paused to strike another, and at the same moment a knock, so quiet and stealthy as to be scarcely audible, sounded on the front door. The matches fell from his hand. He stood motionless, his breath suspended until the knock was repeated. Then he turned and fled swiftly back to his room, and closed the door behind him. A third knock sounded through the house.

'What's that?' cried the old woman, starting up.

'A rat,' said the old man, in shaking tones---a rat. It passed me on the stairs.'

His wife sat up in bed listening. A loud knock resounded through the house. 'It's Herbert!' she screamed. 'It's Herbert!' She ran to the door, but her husband was before her, and catching her by the arm, held her tightly.

'What are you going to do?' he whispered hoarsely.

'It's my boy; it's Herbert!' she cried, struggling mechanically. 'I forgot it was two miles away. What are you holding me for? Let go. I must open the door.'

'For God's sake, don't let it in,' cried the old man trembling.

'You're afraid of your own son,' she cried, struggling. 'Let me go. I'm coming, Herbert; I'm coming.'

There was another knock, and another. The old woman with a sudden wrench broke free and ran from the room. Her husband followed to the landing, and called after her appealingly as she hurried downstairs. He heard the chain rattle back and the bottom bolt drawn slowly and stiffly from the socket. Then the old woman's voice, strained and panting. 'The bolt,' she cried loudly. 'Come down. I can't reach it.'

But her husband was on his hands and knees groping wildly on the floor in search of the paw. If he could only find it before the thing outside got in. A perfect fusillade of knocks reverberated through the house, and he heard the scraping of a chair as his wife put it down in the passage against the door. He heard the creaking of the bolt as it came slowly back, and at the same moment he found the monkey's paw, and frantically breathed his third and last wish. The knocking ceased suddenly, although the echoes of it were still in the house. He heard the chair drawn back and the door opened. A cold wind rushed up the staircase, and a long loud wail of disappointment and misery from his wife gave him courage to run down to her side, and then to the gate beyond. The street lamp flickering opposite shone on a quiet and deserted road.

The Leopard Man's Story
Jack London, 1903

He had a dreamy, far-away look in his eyes, and his sad, insistent voice, gentle-spoken as a maid's, seemed the placid embodiment of some deep-seated melancholy. He was the Leopard Man, but he did not look it. His business in life, whereby he lived, was to appear in a cage of performing leopards before vast audiences, and to thrill those audiences by certain exhibitions of nerve for which his employers rewarded him on a scale commensurate with[41] the thrills he produced.

---

[41] equal or equivalent to

As I say, he did not look it. He was narrow-hipped, narrow-shouldered, and anaemic, while he seemed not so much oppressed by gloom as by a sweet and gentle sadness, the weight of which was as sweetly and gently borne. For an hour I had been trying to get a story out of him, but he appeared to lack imagination. To him there was no romance in his gorgeous career, no deeds of daring, no thrills--nothing but a gray sameness and infinite boredom.

Lions? Oh, yes! he had fought with them. It was nothing. All you had to do was to stay sober. Anybody could whip a lion to a standstill with an ordinary stick. He had fought one for half an hour once. Just hit him on the nose every time he rushed, and when he got artful and rushed with his head down, why, the thing to do was to stick out your leg. When he grabbed at the leg you drew it back and hit hint on the nose again. That was all.

With the far-away look in his eyes and his soft flow of words he showed me his scars. There were many of them, and one recent one where a tigress had reached for his shoulder and gone down to the bone. I could see the neatly mended rents in the coat he had on. His right arm, from the elbow down, looked as though it had gone through a threshing machine, what of the ravage wrought by claws and fangs. But it was nothing, he said, only the old wounds bothered him somewhat when rainy weather came on.

Suddenly his face brightened with a recollection, for he was really as anxious to give me a story as I was to get it.

"I suppose you've heard of the lion-tamer who was hated by another man?" he asked.

He paused and looked pensively at a sick lion in the cage opposite.

"Got the toothache," he explained. "Well, the lion-tamer's big play to the audience was putting his head in a lion's mouth. The man who hated him attended every performance in the hope sometime of seeing that lion crunch down. He followed the show about all over the country. The years went by and he grew old, and the lion-tamer grew old, and the lion grew old. And at last one day, sitting in a front seat, he saw what he had waited for. The lion crunched down, and there wasn't any need to call a doctor."

The Leopard Man glanced casually over his finger nails in a manner which would have been critical had it not been so sad.

"Now, that's what I call patience," he continued, "and it's my style. But it was not the style of a fellow I knew. He was a little, thin, sawed-off, sword-swallowing and juggling Frenchman. De Ville, he called himself, and he had a nice wife. She did trapeze work and used to dive from under the roof into a net, turning over once on the way as nice as you please.

"De Ville had a quick temper, as quick as his hand, and his hand was as quick as the paw of a tiger. One day, because the ring-master called him a frog-eater, or something like that and maybe a little worse, he shoved him against the soft pine background he used in his knife-throwing act, so quick the ring-master didn't have time to think, and there, before the audience, De Ville kept the air on fire with his knives, sinking them into the wood all around the ring-master so close that they passed through his clothes and most of them bit into his skin.

"The clowns had to pull the knives out to get him loose, for he was pinned fast. So the word went around to watch out for De Ville, and no one dared be more than barely civil to his wife. And she was a sly bit of baggage, too, only all hands were afraid of De Ville.

"But there was one man, Wallace, who was afraid of nothing. He was the lion-tamer, and he had the self-same trick of putting his head into the lion's mouth. He'd put it into the mouths of any of them, though he preferred Augustus, a big, good-natured beast who could always be depended upon.

"As I was saying, Wallace--'King' Wallace we called him--was afraid of nothing alive or dead. He was a king and no mistake. I've seen him drunk, and on a wager go into the cage of a lion that'd turned nasty, and without a stick beat him to a finish. Just did it with his fist on the nose.

"Madame de Ville--"

At an uproar behind us the Leopard Man turned quietly around. It was a divided cage, and a monkey, poking through the bars and around the partition, had had its paw seized by a big gray wolf who was trying to pull it off by main strength. The arm seemed stretching out longer end longer like a thick elastic, and the unfortunate monkey's mates were raising a terrible din. No keeper was at hand, so the Leopard Man stepped over a couple of paces, dealt the wolf a sharp blow on the nose with the light cane he carried, and returned with a sadly apologetic smile to take up his unfinished sentence as though there had been no interruption.

"--looked at King Wallace and King Wallace looked at her, while De Ville looked black. We warned Wallace, but it was no use. He laughed at us, as he laughed at De Ville one day when he shoved De Ville's head into a bucket of paste because he wanted to fight.

"De Ville was in a pretty mess--I helped to scrape him off; but he was cool as a cucumber and made no threats at all. But I saw a glitter in his eyes which I had seen often in the eyes of wild beasts, and I went out of my way to give Wallace a final warning. He laughed, but he did not look so much in Madame de Ville's direction after that.

"Several months passed by. Nothing had happened and I was beginning to think it all a scare over nothing. We were West by that time, showing in 'Frisco. It was during the afternoon performance, and the big tent was filled with women and children, when I went looking for Red Denny, the head canvas-man, who had walked off with my pocket-knife.

"Passing by one of the dressing tents I glanced in through a hole in the canvas to see if I could locate him. He wasn't there, but directly in front of me was King Wallace, in tights, waiting for his turn to go on with his cage of performing lions. He was watching with much amusement a quarrel between a couple of trapeze artists. All the rest of the people in the dressing tent were watching the same thing, with the exception of De Ville whom I noticed staring at Wallace with undisguised hatred. Wallace and the rest were all too busy following the quarrel to notice this or what followed.

"But I saw it through the hole in the canvas. De Ville drew his handkerchief from his pocket, made as though to mop the sweat from his face with it (it was a hot day), and at the same time walked past Wallace's back. The look troubled me at the time, for not only did I see hatred in it, but I saw triumph as well.

"'De Ville will bear watching,' I said to myself, and I really breathed easier when I saw him go out the entrance to the circus

grounds and board an electric car for down town. A few minutes later I was in the big tent, where I had overhauled Red Denny. King Wallace was doing his turn and holding the audience spellbound. He was in a particularly vicious mood, and he kept the lions stirred up till they were all snarling, that is, all of them except old Augustus, and he was just too fat and lazy and old to get stirred up over anything.

"Finally Wallace cracked the old lion's knees with his whip and got him into position. Old Augustus, blinking good-naturedly, opened his mouth and in popped Wallace's head. Then the jaws came together, crunch, just like that."

The Leopard Man smiled in a sweetly wistful fashion, and the far-away look came into his eyes.

"And that was the end of King Wallace," he went on in his sad, low voice. "After the excitement cooled down I watched my chance and bent over and smelled Wallace's head. Then I sneezed."

"It . . . it was . . .?" I queried with halting eagerness.

"Snuff--that De Ville dropped on his hair in the dressing tent. Old Augustus never meant to do it. He only sneezed."

How It Happened

Arthur Conan Doyle, 1913

She was a writing medium. This is what she wrote:—

I can remember some things upon that evening most distinctly, and others are like some vague, broken dreams. That is what makes it so difficult to tell a connected story. I have no idea now what it was that had taken me to London and brought me back so late. It just merges into all my other visits to London. But from the time that I got out at the little country station everything is extraordinarily clear. I can live it again—every instant of it.

I remember so well walking down the platform and looking at the illuminated clock at the end which told me that it was half-past eleven. I remember also my wondering whether I could get home before midnight. Then I remember the big motor, with its glaring headlights and glitter of polished brass, waiting for me outside. It was my new thirty-horse-power Robur, which had only been delivered that day. I remember also asking Perkins, my chauffeur, how she had gone, and his saying that he thought she was excellent.

"I'll try her myself," said I, and I climbed into the driver's seat.

"The gears are not the same," said he. "Perhaps, sir, I had better drive."

"No; I should like to try her," said I.

And so we started on the five-mile drive for home.

My old car had the gears as they used always to be in notches on a bar. In this car you passed the gear-lever through a gate to get on the higher ones. It was not difficult to master, and soon I thought that I understood it. It was foolish, no doubt, to begin to learn a new system in the dark, but one often does foolish things, and one has not always to pay the full price for them. I got along very well until I came to Claystall Hill. It is one of the worst hills in England, a mile and a half long and one in six in places, with three fairly sharp curves. My park gate stands at the very foot of it upon the main London road.

We were just over the brow of this hill, where grade is steepest, when the trouble began. I had been on the top speed, and wanted to get her on the free; but she stuck between gears, and I had to get her back on the top again. By this time she was going at a great rate, so I clapped on both brakes, and one after the other they gave way. I didn't mind so much when I felt my footbrake snap, but when I put all my weight on my side-brake, and the lever clanged to its full limit without a catch, it brought a cold sweat out of me. By this time we were fairly tearing down the slope. The lights were brilliant, and I brought her round the first curve all right. Then we did the second one, though it was a close shave for the ditch. There was a mile of straight then with the third curve beneath it, and after that the gate of the park. If I could shoot into that harbour all would be well, for the slope up to the house would bring her to a stand.

Perkins behaved splendidly. I should like that to be known. He was perfectly cool and alert. I had thought at the very beginning of taking the bank, and he read my intention.
"I wouldn't do it, sir," said he. "At this pace it must go over and we should have it on the top of us."

Of course he was right. He got to the electric switch and had it off, so we were in the free; but we were still running at a fearful pace. He laid his hands on the wheel.

"I'll keep her steady," said he, "if you care to jump and chance it. We can never get round that curve. Better jump, sir."
"No," said I; "I'll stick it out. You can jump if you like."
"I'll stick it with you, sir," said he.

If it had been the old car I should have jammed the gear-lever into the reverse, and seen what would happen. I expect she would have stripped her gears or smashed up somehow, but it would have been a chance. As it was, I was helpless. Perkins tried to climb across, but you couldn't do it going at that pace. The wheels were whirring like a 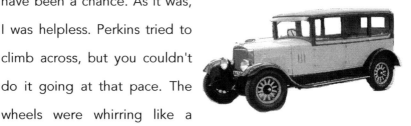 high wind and the big body creaking and groaning with the strain. But the lights were brilliant, and one could steer to an inch. I remember thinking what an awful and yet majestic sight we should appear to anyone who met us. It was a narrow road, and we were just a great, roaring, golden death to anyone who came in our path.

We got round the corner with one wheel three feet high upon the bank. I thought we were surely over, but after staggering for a moment she righted and darted onwards. That was the third corner and the last one. There was only the park gate now. It was facing us, but, as luck would have it, not facing us directly. It was about twenty yards to the left up the main road into which we ran. Perhaps I could have done it, but I expect that the steering-gear had been jarred when we ran on the bank. The wheel did not turn easily. We shot out of the lane. I saw the open gate on the left. I whirled round my wheel with all the strength of my wrists. Perkins and I threw our bodies across, and then the next instant, going at fifty miles an hour, my right wheel struck full on the right-hand pillar of my own gate. I heard the crash. I was conscious of flying through the air, and then—and then —!

When I became aware of my own existence once more I was among some brushwood in the shadow of the oaks upon the lodge side of the drive. A man was standing beside me. I imagined at first that it was Perkins, but when I looked again I saw that it was Stanley, a man whom I had known at college some years before, and for whom I had a really genuine affection. There was always something peculiarly sympathetic to me in Stanley's personality; and I was proud to think that I had some similar influence upon him. At the present moment I was surprised to see him, but I was like a man in a dream, giddy and shaken and quite prepared to take things as I found them without questioning them.

"What a smash!" I said. "Good Lord, what an awful smash!"
He nodded his head, and even in the gloom I could see that he was smiling the gentle, wistful smile which I connected with him.

I was quite unable to move. Indeed, I had not any desire to try to move. But my senses were exceedingly alert. I saw the wreck of the motor lit up by the moving lanterns. I saw the little group of people and heard the hushed voices: There were the lodge-keeper and his wife, and one or two more. They were taking no notice of me, but were very busy round the car. Then suddenly I heard a cry of pain.

"The weight is on him. Lift it easy," cried a voice.
"It's only my leg!" said, another one, which I recognised as Perkins's. "Where's master?" he cried.
"Here I am," I answered, but they did not seem to hear me. They were all bending over something which lay in front of the car.

Stanley laid his hand upon my shoulder, and his touch was inexpressibly soothing. I felt light and happy, in spite of all.
"No pain, of course?" said he.
"None," said I.
"There never is," said he.

And then suddenly a wave of amazement passed over me. Stanley! Stanley! Why, Stanley had surely died of enteric[42] at Bloemfontein in the Boer War!

"Stanley!" I cried, and the words seemed to choke my throat—

---

[42] a stomach disease

"Stanley, you are dead."

He looked at me with the same old gentle, wistful smile.

"So are you," he answered.

Teaching ideas and resources

- New endings

- Climax points

- Mood and atmosphere

- Storyboards

- A sense of place

- Write into a gap

- Changing the perspective

- Modernise a story

- Splitting and sharing

- Monsters, villains and heroes

- What are the key features of a hero?

- Making a monster or villain

- Tracing developmental arcs

- Examining common patterns

- Investigating other stories

- Comparing films and stories

- Further suggestions

Writing stories helps pupils to appreciate reading stories. Reading stories feeds further reading and is the best stimulus for the writing of stories. Both activities nurture those two most precious qualities, empathy for others and creativity. These stories offer myriad opportunities for creative engagement. You'll find places where the stories can be stopped and **new endings** written. How about stopping reading *Bluebeard*, for instance, at the point at which the young bride is first given the key to the one locked door she must not enter? The pupils' task is to finish the story in any way they see fit. This exercise has the extra benefit of creating suspense – pupils have to wait until everyone has written an ending before reading how the original concludes – and of creating extra interest in this resolution. It also provides a way into discussing how stories should and do end.

Climax points in stories are also particularly fun to write. Stopping Theseus as he enters the minotaur's labyrinth and writing the next section will excite many pupils. Or you could join Ichabod Crane in the spooky woods when he hears the pounding of a horse's hooves. More sophisticated writers might be challenged to convey **mood and atmosphere**, generating suspense within the labyrinth's airless confines. Try starting the scene as if it is a still photograph [using spooky photographs of graveyards and haunted houses works a treat]. Less confident writers could be asked to **storyboard** either as an end in itself or as a gateway to extended writing. Or, indeed, the most artistically talented might create a graphic novel style version of one of the stories.

Creating **a sense of place** is crucial to the generation of mood and atmosphere and these stories offer a rich range of settings. Be the police inspectors describing the room in *The Tell-Tale Heart* or Ichabod Crane describing the gloom of the deep woods at night, or the young bride in *Bluebeard* describing with wonder her new husband's fantastical mansion. Or describe what it's like to be lost anywhere when you're a young child.

Or you could break into a story at another point and **write into the gap** you've created. **Change the perspective**, add an extra scene like one deleted from the movie version of the story or reveal what happened in a scene glossed over in the original. Switch narrative technique - write the whole scene through dialogue or interior monologue. For example, re-write *Hansel and Gretel* from the witch's point of view. Describe the crash *in How it Happened* from Perkins' perspective or Bacchus' thoughts and preparations for the arrival of Pentheus.

Hollywood is awash with re-boots and re-mixes of old stories.

Take a leaf from their book and **modernise one of these stories**. What would be the modern equivalent, for instance, of the land where no-one ever dies? Cryonics perhaps or loading our lives onto social media. Or go further, change the genre as well as the temporal setting. What might a sci-fi version of *Theseus and the Minotaur* be like? Or going further still, try mashing up the stories. What would happen if Morgan le Fay crash-landed in the story of Bluebeard? Or if the foolish couple from *The Three Wishes* found themselves being chased by the headless horseman? Watching the Guardian's award winning commercial of *The Three Little Pigs* illustrates the creative power of reinterpretation:

https://www.youtube.com/watch?v=vDGrfhJH1P4]

Splitting and sharing a story so that it's re-written by a class can also be a fun and productive exercise. Working individually or in pairs pupils write a short scene telling their part of the story from a particular point of view. Oscar Wilde's story, *The Very Selfish Giant*, for instance, could be told by an omniscient narrator, then the giant himself, by the children who play in his garden, by the Frost and his pals who bring winter, by the birds and the trees, by the giant again and then finally by the one small child whose story it really is. If there are insufficient perspectives two groups could write competing versions of their character's take on events. That should facilitate some interesting comparative and critical discussion.

Monsters, villains and heroes are always vivid characters that catch children's imaginations. Who can forget the child-catcher in *Chitty Chitty Bang Bang*? In our experience pupils enjoy thinking and writing about and illustrating these kind of characters. Examine them more closely. Collect images of them or clips or extracts. **What are the key features of a hero**? Do they have to be physically strong or handsome? What about a heroine? Does she have to be clever and beautiful? Which of the protagonists in these stories is the most heroic? Which the least? If we produced top trump cards for heroes and monsters what would the various categories be? **Make up your own monster or villain**. A properly terrifying one or the comical sort. Now describe it/them closely, as if you are studying them carefully, going about doing whatever monstrous/villainous thing they normally go about doing. Now have them look up. And see you. What happens next?

Generally we believe that at key stage 3 English teachers should promote creativity and fun over developing analytical skills, although, of course, these are not necessarily contradictory aims. Promoting the enjoyment of reading and writing will in due time lead to the development of critical interest in characters, settings, narrative technique and all the amazing stuff that can be done with language. This way round analytic interest can develop naturally and be sustained.

Focusing still on characters, you might also trace the **developmental arc** the stories' protagonists travel, the barriers or challenges they face, the helper and hinderers they meet along the way. Or you could trace the frequency with which patterns of three crop up, most obviously in the trope of the three wishes. From this could be developed pupils' own three wish stories, or stories of characters who have to face their worst fears in order to grow-up.

Examining various common patterns of narrative, characters and repeated features, or tropes, found in these stories links analysis to creativity. This examination may, indeed, lead to interesting speculation about the ideal ingredients for a great story and some sense of the order in which they need to be arranged for success - a recipe as well as an ingredients list. You could start, for example, with plotting the events in some of the stories along a diagram with time on the x axis and tension on the y, as in the diagram on the following page. Labelling key aspects, such as situation, complication, crisis, climax and resolution can help reveal universal underlying narrative patterns as well as any interesting deviations from the conventional patterns:

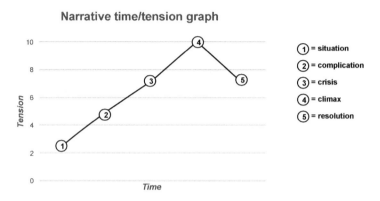

Narrative time/tension graph

1 = situation
2 = complication
3 = crisis
4 = climax
5 = resolution

Stories lead on to other stories. Reading the two Greek myths included in this anthology might encourage pupils to **investigate others**. For starters we recommend *Orpheus and Eurydice* [which will appear in volume 2], *Perseus and the Gorgons* and the less well known story of *Phaeton* – a story crying out for a modern version where the young man borrows his father's private jet. A particularly rich source for less familiar stories in Ted Hughes' peerless *Tales from Ovid* on which we leaned a little for our version of the Pentheus story.

Hollywood has also drawn deeply from the magic cup of Greek stories. Pupils usually enjoy watching Jason battling with the skeletons, however antiquated the CGI may be. And there's the

Percy Jackson series of books and films as well as the under-rated *Clash of the Titans* with its terrific giant scorpion battle scene.

And it's not just Greek myths. With Odin one-eye, the strong but not terribly bright thunder God, Thor, and the treacherous trickster god, Loki, Asgard, bifrost and the land of the giants, The Norse stories are nearly as rich and have also recently featured in watchable recent films.

Comparing films and stories is always fun and instructive about the resources, capabilities and limits of both media. Films, of course, are especially strong on visuals and on action. For those of a robust constitution, and certainly not for key stage 3 pupils, there is Tim Burton's splendidly gothic [and bloody] version of *Sleepy Hollow*. Perhaps though a year 9 class would be able to cope with the first scene. An interesting comparison with Conan Doyle's story is the Spanish director Alejandro Amenabar's claustrophobic *The Others*, which shares the same narrative twist. As a depiction of neurosis it could also be compared to Poe's tale. What would be the challenges of turning some of the other Victorian stories such as Poe's into films? How might a director convey the mind of the protagonist in *The Tell-Tale Heart*, for instance?

Further suggestions for teaching

1. Ways of reading the stories:

   - Keep it varied and interactive: whole class; small groups; paired readers; individuals.

   - The whole class does not necessarily need to read the same story at the same time. There is much to be gained by giving different groups different stories and then discussing, as a class, a particular aspect such as structure or the presentation of character.

   - Give pupils some choice - provide a selection of, say, 3 openings/ first sentences. Pupils individually or in groups choose the one they prefer and justify their choice [voice, setting, language]. They can then read the one that they have chosen from the selection.

   - If at all possible occasionally, organise a space for story telling rather than individuals behind desks.

   - Pupils do not always initially require the text. For example, listening to Poe's *The Tell-Tale Heart* in the dark, read by torchlight can be suitably dramatic.

   - Consider introducing, first, short pertinent quotations from the story you are considering. Students then assess these in terms of, for example, mood, imagery, style, and impression of character.

2. Speaking and Listening:

The opportunities for group, pair and whole class work are limitless. Here are a few ideas:

- Write and record a radio play of, for example, an *Aesop's Fable*. Pupils will need to think about adapting the story, tone of voice, sound effects.
- Create a movie trailer for a production of, for example, *Bluebeard* (Year 9).
- Put a character on trial - choose one of the villains from the stories, or one of the more morally ambiguous characters (the giant, the father of *Hansel and Gretel*, the fox) and create a formal trial scenario - a group for the defence, a group for the prosecution, judge and jury.
- Hot seat characters and ask them to justify their actions.

About the authors

Head of English and freelance writer, Neil Bowen has a Masters Degree in Literature & Education from Cambridge University and is a member of Ofqual's experts panel for English. He is the author of *The Art of Writing English Essays for GCSE*, co-author of *The Art of Writing English Essays for A-level and Beyond* and of *The Art of Poetry*, volumes 1-5. Neil runs the peripeteia project, bridging the gap between A-level and degree level English courses: www.peripeteia.webs.com.

Janice Gearon is an experienced English teacher with an MA in American Literature. Janice has a particular interest in The History of Art and expertise in fiction for children and for teenage readers.

Printed in Great Britain
by Amazon